Global Dimensions: The Super 7 of Global Success

TRESTÉ LOVING

www.TotalPublishingAndMedia.com

DEDICATIONS

First, I dedicate this book to my loving, amazing, caring, husband, Scott, who has supported me in all my endeavors. He believes in me and reminds me of my past successes which he witnessed. When I needed a push, Scott provided it by keeping me on track with my business or my health. Scott is my dream and I love him with all that I am.

I also dedicate this book to Scott Benning, my mentor aboard the USS George Washington. He allowed me to develop my leadership skills and he was there when I needed a little course correction. He provided me with the right amount of praise and an appropriate amount of discipline, which helped me advance in rank. Scott allowed me to be myself and that's powerful! Thanks, Scott!

My final dedication is to my little brother, Marvin. He lost his battle against cancer in October 2013. Although Marvin knew his prognosis, he was amazing and a true inspiration to me. He was always more concerned about my health than his own no matter how he was feeling. I learned a different type of courage and strength from him and that's why I dedicate this book to Marvin. Marvin, you'll always be with me and I'll love you always.

TABLE OF CONTENTS

Acknowledgments vii

Why Read This Book ix

You Want This Book If xi

Introduction – The Q & A Format xiii

Part I - The 7 Global Business Imperatives ... 1

Chapter 1: Socialization - What is socialization? 3
Chapter 2: Diversity - Why is it so important? 16
Chapter 3: Teams - How are team members selected? 25
Chapter 4: Intent versus Impact - How does it happen? 31
Chapter 5: Diamond Perspective - How many
           perspectives do people have? 37
Chapter 6: Race - What is behind race? 43
Chapter 7: Communications - The simple
           communication process 49

Part II - Ellen Torbert ... 59

Core Concept 1: Diversity at 32,000 feet
Core Concept 2: How does an organization get started?
Core Concept 3: Designer Fit
Core Concept 4: What are others saying?
Core Concept 5: What's next?

Part III - Scott Benning ... 67

Core Concept 1: Global Force For Good
Core Concept 2: Why Navy Equals Opportunity
Core Concept 3: Mission Accomplished
Core Concept 4: Chain of Command
Core Concept 5: Anchors Aweigh on Diversity/Inclusion

Part IV - Renée Fuller ... 75

Core Concept 1: Partner in Law
Core Concept 2: Unique Perspectives
Core Concept 3: How she impacted others
Core Concept 4: Man she can talk
Core Concept 5: A quiet storm

Part V - Gary Hill ... 81

Core Concept 1: Facilitation Saves the Nation
Core Concept 2: How does she do it?
Core Concept 3: Leader among leaders
Core Concept 4: Can you trust her?
Core Concept 5: She's got talent

Part VI - Dee Buie ... 89

Core Concept 1: What a difference she makes
Core Concept 2: Three sides to every story
Core Concept 3: Strictly business
Core Concept 4: Adaptive leadership
Core Concept 5: Never judge a book

Conclusion 97

About The Author 99

ACKNOWLEDGMENTS

I acknowledge Ellen Torbert, Scott Benning, Reneé Fuller, Gary Hill, and Dee Buie for giving their time and valuable honest assessment of me and my work. You guys rock! I also acknowledge my family who encourages me to do new things and keeps me moving using some old Kentucky sayings. They also make me laugh.

WHY READ THIS BOOK

No one is alike save identical twins, but, they only look alike. That's why this book is important to you as a CEO or Business Owner. Each of your employees are different, even if they are the same race, ethnic group, sex, religion, culture, age, speak the same language, on and on. CEOs and Business Owners will find that the uniqueness of each employee is what really leads to increased productivity, reduced conflict, advanced customer service, heightened talent retention, and more. This book gives CEOs and Business Owners a way to integrate their employee's unique attributes and diversity in order to achieve business objectives, new out-of-the-box ideas, and a team-based environment where employees work together to accomplish the mission and vision of the organization.

The global market demands that organizations understand the uniqueness of each culture and this book provides the dimensions needed to be phenomenal globally, nationally, and locally. This book will be the key diversity source for CEOs, Business Owners, and Senior Executives.

YOU WANT THIS BOOK IF...

→ You do business globally and want to make a momentous impact on the market.

→ Your organization is working on their first diversity strategy.

→ You are a CEO or Business Owner who wants to create a more productive, talent-rich, inclusive culture.

→ You are a Business Owner or CEO who desires straight answers to difficult and uneasy topics.

→ You are a CEO or Business Owner who wants to learn new concepts that inspire a positive work environment.

INTRODUCTION – THE Q & A FORMAT

This book is in a Q & A format. CEOs and Business Owners will find this format clear and precise. It focuses the reader on the topic, thereby keeping their attention. The questions in this book are based on real experiences. Therefore, the answers are proven results or what should have happened but did not because leaders chose not to take suggested actions. When discussing race, diversity, and better communications, the Q & A format provides Business Owners and CEOs with a quick reference versus reading numerous pages to get an answer or an idea.

Additionally, the Q & A format allows readers to use this book as a convenient tool for understanding organization issues while using other filters, talking points from executive meetings, or any other situations a CEO or Business Owner deems applicable.

There are also interviews, Parts II through VI, with colleagues who describe Tresté's work, her experience, knowledge and talents, as well as how valuable she would be to any organization.

Readers will be hard-pressed to find a more direct, experience-based, out-of-the-box thinking collection of global business imperatives.

PART I
THE 7 GLOBAL BUSINESS IMPERATIVES

1 SOCIALIZATION

Q: My name is Scott and I am the Interviewer.

A: Hi, I'm Tresté Loving and I am the Author.

Q: Please introduce yourself.

A: Hello, I'm Tresté Loving and I help CEOs and Business Owners maneuver through this diverse, dynamic, virtual, global-driven world to make smarter, quicker, informed business decisions - so they can sleep at night.

Q: What will your target audience discover by reading this book?

A: Readers will get so much. The main thing they will take away is how important diversity and inclusion strategies are to their organization. Once they develop those diversity and inclusion strategies, they will actually be a global force in their industry and often in other industries as well.

Q: **Core Concept 1:** Socialization - what is socialization?

A: Socialization is the process of growing up and learning who you are. There are so many influencers to the socialization process. One of the big ones for the Gen Y and/or millennial are media outlets; everything is media-related - the games they grew up playing, the movies they watch, their telephones and their iPads. These are all huge influences on them because they fulfill their 'I need it now syndrome'. When Gen Y joins an organization or business, they maintain that same mentality - I need it now. The technology they use before they enter the job market is the same technology they take with them to the job market. That often becomes a huge issue and causes divisiveness in the work place.

The work environment, organization, and/or business must have their own socialization process. In my past experience as a diversity officer (because there are five generations in the workplace

3

now), I know they don't have a socialization process. Combining generations is crucial to the work environment. It takes time, a lot of talking and the willingness on everyone's part to give a little. It ultimately creates the most awesome organization.

In the past, I have taken small groups from each generation and formed a work group so they could talk out their issues and see things from someone else's perspective. Once they did that, they discovered things about each other they didn't know before; they had just assumed. After this exercise, they were willing to work together to demonstrate how they function to the other generations, and explain why they work the way they do. They actually came up with ideas on their own to work better together.

This is just one small thing to do and it doesn't take a lot of time. Once they start working on it together, it just becomes a natural thing.

Putting different generations together and allowing them to create their own socialization process is beneficial to the whole organization. It brings goodwill, positive thinking and creates a work environment in which everyone can thrive.

Q: What impacts the socialization process?

A: As I said earlier, there are many influencers and impacts on the socialization process. One is media, yet there are many more. Parents play a large role in the socialization process, as do religion, friends, schools and teachers. The culture someone is born into also takes a toll.

Socialization is individualistic and employers need to understand their socialization process is the same. While they may have had different top influencers, it is still the same process.

Let me give you an example of the different generations. This is really important and affects the work environment. Look at the baby boomers, and I am one of them; the media did not have a huge impact on how we were socialized.

I remember when there were only three major networks on TV because cable wasn't around. We had ABC, NBC and CBS, and that's all you got. There was an antenna sticking out of the roof and you fiddled with it to make sure you got the best reception. Watching TV was not a big issue.

You didn't watch for many hours because after-school activities were what you were interested in - sports, hobbies, a variety of things. I grew up in Kentucky where there was 4H - 4H was everything.

As I explained earlier, media and technology are now the biggest influencers. Understanding these as major influences helps leaders figure out how they need to set up their socialization processes to successfully transition all who enter their organization. It is important to understand how people are influenced before they become employees of a company.

Q: What influences the socialization process the most?

A: Like I said, media and technology. It's not the Gen Y's fault they were socialized in that way. If both parents were working, the Gen Ys were not expected to get themselves to a soccer game, a Lacrosse game or other after-school activities; this wasn't feasible. They could, however, get themselves home to play a video game, watch TV, or text their friends from their phone.

They used to be called latchkey kids, but that term faded. Now when they're home, they turn to the easiest form of entertainment - an electronic game or the TV.

With the media being the largest influencer, the Gen Ys have an advantage. The world is technology-driven and things get done faster. There are things that were not available to the other generations, those who came before the millennial. This new generation experiences life in the now. They have missed out on things other generations enjoyed. This is a brand new socialization.

Q: How does the media in all its forms impact socialization?

A: Media impacts all the generations now, sometimes in a positive way, sometimes in a negative way. Baby boomers and previous generations have to catch up with the technology and media of today.

They are not necessarily comfortable with the technology that's there. That's why they have a hard time dealing with Gen Y. Gen Y can text, talk on the phone and work at the same time. The older generation's response tends to be: "I can barely deal with this computer. I remember back when you just used paper and pencil." The olden days.

It is important that everyone understands that media can either be a hindrance or one of our greatest tools; one we're going to keep as a society and as a world. People need to adjust to media and move forward with technology.

What I've seen and experienced with different generations is their ease with technology, or lack thereof. You have to strike a balance for everyone involved. The Gen Ys have to throttle back when they're in a work environment where co-workers are not as comfortable with advanced technology. They may become bored and frustrated. Having patience and offering assistance to other generations will help Gen Ys with their boredom. Everyone will feel more comfortable as productivity increases. These are easy steps and involves all generations moving in the same direction.

Using the above example, leaders alleviate frustration between generations by focusing them on tasks and how to accomplish them better. Millennials can learn how to communicate verbally using different communication skills. Socializing an organization through media is essential to making it a global phenomena and force in the marketplace.

Q: Why should leaders be concerned about the socialization process?

A: They need to be concerned because if they don't socialize the employees entering the organization to a new and common theme, people will feel left behind, frustrated, and they will fail organizational expectations.

Not taking uncommon backgrounds into consideration can impact an entire organization. Bringing people with varying knowledge and opinions about certain things into the same place and having them work together without having something in common is a mistake.

Leaders might think that the common denominator is the organization, but that's not always true. They need to socialize them into their organization.

What do I mean by that? The success of a business will rely on a common thread that is drawn throughout the organization, becoming everyone's goal and vision. They should also be on the same training and educational cycle.

Everything should be common to everyone in the organization. They should not be concerned about who they are within the organization, but rather how they fit into it. That commonality is crucial to its success.

So, leaders really have to understand socialization influencers and what it means to socialize everyone to the organization's standards.

Q: How important is socialization to a company?

A: As I said, it can break a business down, cause it to be dysfunctional, keep it from reaching its goals, and prevent it from being a solid company. It will be a group of people trying to work toward their own personal goals rather than the goals of the organization; just there to draw a paycheck, maybe to get some training or an education so they can move on to another organization where they feel they will fit in better.

No one is working for the organization per se; everybody is working for themselves. That is easy to see. I have walked into organizations and felt it. You can feel that there isn't any cohesiveness. You can sense that it's every man or woman for themselves. There's tension, apprehension, and no one is working toward the common good. They don't care about the customers or their clients. They care about themselves. It's really disheartening to see that.

Leaders can sometimes feel hopeless; "I don't know what to do. I'm not sure what I'm not doing. I'm not sure why I'm not doing it." There are ways that leaders can fix this issue but it will take longer than it would have if they had socialized the people to the organization.

There are numerous directions to go in - they can read books, they can search out people who have businesses that can help them in that type of interest, or they can just say, "Hey, we know there's an issue. We're not going to ignore it. We're going to do something about it."

Q: What are some obvious differences between Generation Y and other generations that can be attributed to their socialization process?

A: There are huge differences and there are subtle differences. Subtle differences would include Gen Y's concern about how much time they have for themselves. Gen Y would prefer to not be expected to work a longer shift in order to get the job done. If they were told that their work hours were eight to four, then they're not going to be at work at four or five.

Older generations are loyal to the organization so even if they have the same work hours - eight to four - they are a leader. Their boss might say, "Hey Sally, I'm sorry but we need you to stay for another half hour to 45 minutes," and Sally would reply, "Sure, no problem."

Now, boomers aren't necessarily thrilled about staying late, but they are loyal to the organization to a point. They understand they were hired to work eight to four but they have a life outside of work, so they're probably not going to happily do an extra half hour. Some people don't realize some of the similarities between the generations.

Like I said, those are subtle differences. I have already talked about the major differences - a significant one being their ability to work in the now with the technology and media available to them.

Meetings are another. Gen Y's don't like meetings because they consider it a waste of time. They would prefer to discuss things via text message, on the phone, or in an email. They're not really too fond of meetings.

The baby boomers and older workers prefer face-to-face - I need to see your face when I'm talking to you about this, particularly if it's an issue. That's what they would prefer.

Getting around that means being creative when you're dealing with different groups. There are such big differences. Again, you can appeal to both sides by accommodating both of them rather than just having a meeting. If it's something really simple and quick, let's just say, "I think we should go this way and this is why," it can be sent as a text message. They can respond, "Okay, sounds good." You don't need a meeting for that. The times that you do need a meeting because of its complexity will not be appealing to a Gen Y.

There are different ways people handle issues and there are various resources out there to help leaders. Not all leaders have to use things off the cuff if they really don't know how.

There are videos and DVDs that define meetings. John Cleese is really good with his series, *Meetings, Bloody Meetings*. If you haven't seen them or if you have and it's been a few years, I suggest you pull the series out or buy it and share it with all of your employees. You'll hear a lot of people say, "You're right, we don't need a meeting for this."

Q: How should socialization be used in an organization?

A: It should be used as a tool to bring people together - not to have everyone forming their own socialization process, working as individuals. It will never work if you have an organization of individuals. It will work, however, if you socialize everyone to an organization of people working toward the same goal from a common place.

This is how organizational leaders socialize employees to the same common place; an organization that creates great products, services for their customers and their clients, and a great work environment for their employees. This allows employees to become engaged in the purpose of the organization.

Basically, when a group of people work together in a smooth, silky process, customers and clients become raving fans, and raving fans are the way to keep and get new business.

You want raving fans! Don't forget, fans are great to show, and "fans" is an abbreviation for "fanatics," and there's nothing bad about having someone fanatically support your organization in a good way.

Q: Why is it important to understand the difference between natural and deliberate socialization?

A: Those are the two ways people are socialized. Natural is when you're really, really young and it's inert. People don't even realize - when you're a baby, you're getting socialized; when you're a toddler, you're getting socialized - all that's natural. That's second nature, if you will. It's part of socialization.

Then, when you're eight, nine and ten, the deliberate socialization starts happening. When your parents start taking an active role in socializing you - taking you to church if you're believers, taking you out in social settings and telling you, "Don't put your elbows on the table," "Put your napkin in your lap," "Don't talk so loud," "Chew your food," blah, blah, blah. That's deliberate socialization. That's where that comes from.

It's key to understand when deliberate socialization starts. You're being groomed, if you will, to be the person your parents would love for you to be.

On the other hand, you're also being socialized when you begin hanging out with friends. Your friends may not be the type of people your parents want you to hang out with. They influence you, possibly in different ways.

Deliberate socialization is when you're confused about what's right, what's wrong, why do I do this, why shouldn't I do that, or why don't I do this? It becomes a crap shoot of sorts, where you, as a person, decide what you're going to take on to make you the grown up that you want to be.

It's very difficult when you're in your teens to start making such long-term decisions, but that is when it begins.

Q: What are the results of the socialization process?

A: It's when you start becoming the person you're going to be. When you're in your twenties, you see the results of the socialization process. When you're pre-teen and moving into your teens, you don't think about the decisions you make or how they are going to affect who you are when you're a grown adult. It's always good to have someone you can trust to help make those decisions at that age.

Decisions should not be made or influenced by a friend who is kind of suspect in their behavior, by what they're going to do, or by watching too much inappropriate TV that is going to make a negative impact.

What we do know from the socialization process is that the things teens and preteens start watching and doing, and the people they hang out with definitely influences them. They will pick up those behaviors and words, and unfortunately become that person without something or someone to influence them away from those behaviors.

It's up to parents, grandparents, and other positive influencers in their circle to help them socialize into a better perspective and being so they can make good decisions early on. So, when they do become an adult, they're in a better frame of mind, they're in a better state, and they will be a positive impact on others who are younger or on their own children.

It's important to understand what influences you early and impacts you later.

Q: Is it possible to change someone's results from their socialization?

A: Yes, it is. There is no doubt that it is possible. It does happen. I've seen it happen. There are studies, research, all kinds of things that you can seek out on the web to prove beyond a doubt that how you're initially socialized will hugely impact who you are later.

It is a matter of fact that who we get our values from at a young age (and it's really remarkable how young it is; nine, ten, eleven years old) determines the base set of values we're going to take with us for the rest of our lives.

I was stunned when I first saw the documentation on this. I was like, "there's no way." But, when I started thinking back on my own life, I realized it is true. It is important to know we do not change our values. If we do (on very rare occasion), it is usually caused by what people in my profession call a SEE, a significant emotional event - it does have to be significant.

Unless you're having one SEE after another, your values will remain the same from pre-teen throughout the duration of your life. There's plenty of research to document this. As far as your values are concerned, unless you are having a SEE, you are basically who you're going to be by the time you are eight, nine and ten.

Q: Is there some secret to the socialization process?
A: The only true secret to the socialization process is everyone understanding how you became who you are, and what you can do if, as an adult, you're starting down a path that may not be in your best interest. Someone might see that and say, "Whoa, you need to think about this, think about what you're saying, think about what you are doing, and try to get yourself on a different path." How you say it is very important because you don't want to say, "…on a better path," because someone could take that as an attack. You also don't want to say, "I'm going to make you better," or, "let's get you on a better road," because someone might take offense and think you are attacking them by insinuating that something is wrong. "So, you're saying that there is something wrong with me, the way I am, and the path I am taking?"

Words are critical when you're talking about the socialization process and it's very important for people to understand that words are different. They mean a lot and if you want to affect a particular situation, say something such as, "well, lrt's check out a different pat." You can't necessarily change someone's mind, but you can change his or her perspective.

Q: Is there a training for this process?

A: Yes. Just like anything else, you research the training you've decided to undertake. There's sound, viable training out there. I've done my own research because I train on these topics and have found that there are plenty of good trainings on socialization and the socialization process.

The one thing you have to be careful with is how you word your training. It's not that somebody's wrong in what they're doing - it's about offering something different from what others are doing.

As long as you keep that frame of mind, you can present it to those who require the training and those coming to work for your organization. The most important factor is offering something different; something that will make them totally successful within your organization and in their profession, as well as something that will help them excel in their career. Yes, there is training out there. I would highly recommend utilizing it.

Q: Considering its importance, why isn't this something people talk about?

A: People don't really know a lot about socialization nor do they understand it. It's not a common dinner conversation. It's not a topic that comes up in the work environment.

This is important for leaders to take on and for their organization to show people. This is what we're doing - talking about socialization; this is something good and that's why we're talking about it now.

There aren't a lot of books about socialization because it's one of those things that people don't think of. It affects everyone. To be a successful organization, you need to have a socialization process in your onboarding and as continual training.

Q: Is socialization a conscious or subconscious process?

A: Initially, in the natural socialization process, it's subconscious, and sometimes it remains that way throughout one's life. This is attributed to people not understanding it and not knowing anything about it. As I said, it is not a common subject.

It can, however, be a conscious decision for leaders in the organization when they bring people on board. It needs to be this way so that it can be a conscious decision by their employees as well.

Q: How does an organization's process work?

A: Each organization is going to be different. When I offer socialization training, I start with the "before": how they were socialized as they were growing up. This is so people are on the same page and they have that ah-ha moment; "Wow, that explains a lot. Now I know why I..." or, "I understand what I did." Everyone is caught up.

We then discuss socialization in their work environment and what needs to be done, what should be done, and when it needs to happen - which is now. We go through this process to get them on their way to success, thus making the organization successful, keeping customers and clients satisfied and convinced that it is doing what it should do and will continue to excel.

That's what I provide to an organization when we are talking about the socialization process. I point out bad situations or a lack of socialization, then I point out good situations where socialization has taken place. I take note of where the company was before the process as well as where they stand after adopting their own system. This process should be specific to their own industry, to their particular employees and their basic needs. Your company begins and ends as two totally different organizations, if you will. You recreate your company in the light that you really want.

Q: How important is socialization to an organization?

A: If you don't have a socialization process incorporated in your business, you may be slightly successful. However, you won't do as well as a similar organization that has these processes instilled. Your employees are all there as individuals who happen to be in the same place at the same time, but they're not necessarily working together. They're coming from 5,000 different backgrounds and perspectives based on their upbringing rather than the company's values.

That's what the true key is. It's 5,000 people working from the same perspective, from the organization's perspective - that's what leaders need.

Q: Who influences an organization's socialization process?

A: First, the CEO and/or business owner. They have to be on board with socialization. They have to show their socialization process to the organization so that employees can see how committed they are to both the values and the people they are socializing - for the greater good of the organization, their customers and clients, and their suppliers.

This is what the CEOs and Business Owners must show in their behavior, and must speak every time they are in both formal and informal settings. When they happen to be walking around among their employees, they should be talking organization - organization is socialization. That's what they have to do in order to make their business as successful as possible.

For example, if the CEO is not interested in socializing his or her business, then they are just a figurehead. That CEO means nothing to that organization unless he or she backs a total socialization process of their company, them included. Once that happens, their employees see someone different. Their employees see someone who's actually in the organization with them and not just a figurehead above them.

Q: How can leaders figure out their socialization process?

A: In order for leaders to learn the socialization process, they need to know who is establishing it. That person must know the organization inside and out

Once that person is chosen, he/she has to be strong enough to talk to the CEO or business owner and advise them about what isn't going on, where they are failing, and where they are barely holding onto their customers and clients.

Then, I recommend actions needed to get the company together through a socialization process that will unite them so that they are working toward the same goals, mission and vision. They will eventually be able to show success not only in some empirical matter, but most importantly in statistical data (before and after numbers).

That will persuade the leaders to get on board. Once the leaders are on board. it's like magic. Everybody follows in line.

One saying that I learned in the Navy (and it's appropriate in the Navy or out of it), is that what interests your leader, fascinates you. That's what you need to keep in mind when you're developing your socialization process and trying to bring everybody onboard.

Q: Who should be responsible for the organization's socialization process?

A: Sounds like a repeat doesn't it?

2 DIVERSITY

Q: **Core Concept 2:** Diversity - why is it so important?

A: Diversity now - we are truly global. There is nothing that divides us. Oceans used to divide us. The oceans are still there, but just symbolically. They don't keep us from doing business. They don't stop us from providing products and services to anyone, anywhere.

What that means is that someone who has a business in Iowa, for example, has to be able to expand their marketing in order to communicate their products and services, their quality, and how they could benefit customers and clients in Nepal. The only way they're going to be able to do that is to understand Nepal's market, and that's diversity.

So, the global workforce and marketplace is right here in the U.S. as well. We have different races, ethnicities, religions and even ages. We don't have to go outside our country to find diversity in our marketplace. You have to understand diversity to be able to be successful.

Q: Does diversity only include race, ethnicity, religion and culture?

A: Definitely not. We have tried to pigeonhole diversity to fit certain criteria but it   encompasses differences and that's exactly what it means - diverse means different. We're different in all kinds of ways. Diversity does not just include the, as I call it, "obvious diversity" that you can see. It goes much further. Diversity has many dimensions.

Q: An all- Caucasian male work environment isn't diverse, is it?

A: An all-Caucasian male working environment is just as diverse as one you can see the differences in. Let me give you an example that was actually brought up to me by someone else. He just said, "I can't believe all I didn't know about diversity and inclusion." I told him, "Well, you're not alone. I'm glad that I provided you with something that you could understand." He said, "But I don't have to worry about diversity because our group of people are all Caucasian males. We're not diverse." I said, "Oh, no, no, no, you're very diverse."

I asked him a couple of questions. I asked him if everyone in his work environment was from the same state or part of the country and he said, "No." I asked him, "Are all of you the same age?" he said, "No." I said, "So, you already answered two questions that make your work environment diverse. He looked at me and respondes, "Your'e right." It's true; everyone is diverse. We're all different from another. Even if we look the same, it does not mean we are the same. That's a key to understanding diversity and its important in the work environment.

17

Q: Only minorities should be diversity directors, vice presidents or officers, right?

A: No. Unfortunately, though, if you searched out diversity officers in Fortune 500 companies, you would see the majority of them are minorities. That poses the question of "why?" Surprisingly, most organizations feel a minority should be the diversity officer because he/she would have the most understanding of it. I mean, aren't they the best option because they are a minority? No. Not true.

The assumption that only a minority could understand a minority issue is almost ludicrous. A diversity officer needs to be strong, they need to fully understand the concepts of diversity and inclusion. They need to be able to communicate across the organization and influence people.

They must have the ability to persuade the CEO and/or business owner and the most junior employees that what they're doing will pay off, it will benefit everyone - not just minorities. It will benefit everyone in the organization.

Sometimes just picking minorities for that position sends the wrong message.

Q: How effective can a Caucasian male be as a diversity VP?

A: The Caucasian male as a diversity officer is priceless. The reason why: too many Caucasian males believe that they don't really have to be involved in diversity and that it is only for minorities. That is just ludicrous. I've already given the example that a white male is diverse. There's no need to categorize them - they are diverse.

There's a term, the "white male club," that is used because they have privileges; privileges that some of them don't know about and others do not care to have. The white male club is powerful. Most organizations, even Fortune 500 companies, are run by white males. A white male in the diversity officer role must ensure that diversity programs are good.

Q: Isn't diversity just another word for affirmative action?

A: No. People don't fully understand affirmative action. Unfortunately, affirmative action went awry quickly, and no one is truly at fault. I think it's important to understand they are two different things: affirmative action is still a part of Title Seven and it still has to be followed in organizations. There's a report every year that's part of the Equal Employment Opportunity Report. Affirmative action is still something that's actionable and it needs to be reported on.

So, diversity and affirmative action are two different things, they function in different ways, and they have different missions.

Q: Could you explain the difference between affirmative action and diversity?

A: Yes. Diversity is not a law. There is one executive order that President Obama signed in 2008. It's like an in- the- air suggestion that organizations do the best they can to ensure people have the opportunities they deserve based on merit. That's what we should have all been doing, basing everything on merit.

The Affirmative Action Policy is a law and it's administered through the Equal Employment Opportunity Council. It was meant to level things out for minorities. For example: When you have a majority member, which we referred to as Caucasian, and you have a minority, which is everyone that's not a Caucasian, and they're applying for the same position, all things must be equal.

In this situation, you can have a majority member and a minority member with the same good rankings and qualifications for the job, on the job they received the same annual evaluations, their education is comparable and they have worked in the same types of positions.

Considering that almost everything is equal with the only difference being that one is a minority and one is the majority member, the leader can choose the minority if that is appropriate. The reason why he can choose the minority is because of past misdeeds, if you will, where minorities weren't advanced because they were a minority. This is what they try to call "leveling the playing field." Giving minorities a slight advantage to be advanced in organizations so their representation in such leadership positions become equal with majority members.

That's the difference. That's why there is still affirmative action policies that have to be reviewed to make sure that when it's possible and feasible, minorities are given advancement opportunities.

What happened with affirmative action, though, is leaders started to advance minorities who were unqualified, who were not equal, if you will, to the majority members. They ended up with minority members in positions they were not qualified for, they didn't know anything about, and they displayed poor performance in. Leaders said, "See, I did what I was supposed to do with affirmative action but they can't even do the job." 'They' meaning minorities.

So, that's how affirmative action started getting a bad name and people started not following it at all.

Q: How useful are diversity practices and policies?

A: When the diversity practice and/or policy makes sense and it does not give a minority an unfair advantage over others, then they're very useful. It inspires minorities. It inspires everyone to want to do their best, to be their best and to give their all to the company for which they work. They become faithful and committed. When you have committed individuals in an organization, they become engaged and you can't stop an organization with engaged employees - they will excel.

Q: Isn't diversity just about numbers?

A: No, diversity is not just about numbers. Sometimes it appears to be, but it is not, and any organization that is focusing on that is not practicing diversity. They're practicing affirmative action in the wrong way. Diversity is about merit. Diversity is about how well people do their job and advance. We're not trying to reach a quota of 20% minorities in leadership positions. That's not what it is meant to do. It is meant to advance those who have the skills, the talents, the abilities, the knowledge and unique perspectives to the positions where they should be.

Q: When is there too much diversity?

A: It seems like that wouldn't be an issue but it really is. You can have too many people in the wrong place and without the right skills. That is too much diversity. Trying to reach a quota, a self-imposed quota, can damage the work environment because you have too many people in the wrong place and without the right skills. That is not a formula for success.

Q: Who should lead an organization's diversity efforts?

A: CEOs and Business Owners must lead the diversity program - they must speak it, they must walk it, and they must talk it everywhere they go within and outside of the organization, in addition to having a public forum they can speak to; those should be the top things they talk about - people can really see it. They're enthusiastic about it. They're emotional about it. They're committed to their organization and their diversity and inclusion programs. The CEOs and the Business Owners have to be committed.

It goes back to what I said before: if your leader is interested in it, then everyone else must be fascinated with it.

Q: How should leaders develop their diversity policies?

A: They need to be wise about what diversity can do for an organization, for their organization. They must pick the right people to help lead their diversity program, not just a VP or a director of diversity. They need senior managers, mid-level managers, and first line supervisors to all be onboard, including employees. They need help with developing these policies and strategies.

They should definitely lead it but they need others completely committed to it as well. This is an organizational policy. It's not just a leader-led policy.

Q: What must be included in diversity policies?

A: One thing - their diversity policy and strategy have to be linked with the business strategy in every way. That's really what it is; a business strategy with different aspects to it. It has to include things like accountability for certain items that are in the policy. It has to be followed up with.

There also needs to be benchmarking to make sure that the diversity strategy is actually working. There has to be senior managers who are in charge of certain items. It has to be department run, including operations, safety, maintenance, etc. It's very involved and not just an overarching policy. It's one that needs to be vetted throughout the entire organization.

Q: How should an organization's diversity program be communicated?

A: It must be communicated in various forms - written, spoken, and through behaviors, starting with the CEO and business owner. When they speak about it, they have to be passionate. It can't be, "We have a great diversity program here." No. They need to give some examples and make it felt.

For example, "Our diversity programs and strategies are the best I've been around. They far exceed my realm. They are the most awesome programs I've experienced. I'm so proud of where we are and I'm looking forward to how far we can take this." Something to that effect.

It also should be displayed formally and informally. As the CEO or business owner walks throughout the organization, he/she should   talk about it and ask for ideas, "What can we do better in our diversity programs?" and, "What do you see?" and, "My door is always open," or, "Please communicate your concerns and ideas to my VP of diversity." That should be how it's communicated throughout the business.

If the organization has a newsletter, the CEO or business owner should have something in there about diversity and where they see the organization going - incorporating quotes and testimonials.

It's important to be communicated effectively, with passion, and they should always ask people for ideas.

Q: What are the dimensions of diversity?

A: There are so many dimensions. I'm going to key in on a few that we haven't talked about: intelligence, culture, thinking styles, and different languages, as well as the way they use their language to support the organization in the global marketplace. I know I mentioned religion but it is religion as a dimension.

There are a wide variety of dimensions. In the cultural dimensions, it's how people view situations from their personal cultural dimensions. We all view the same things from different perspectives based on our culture.

So, again, it's not just what we see; it's the things that make us who we are, and those are the dimensions that we bring. Male/female - although we can see it, we approach different subjects differently and that's a dimension of our culture. I'll give a couple of examples here:

Males don't mind being aggressive when they're presenting their ideas. Women try not to be aggressive and try to settle things in a more subtle manner. We don't have to get in each other's faces to settle something. In the Asian culture, it is not common for things to be settled in dispute. As they say, they prefer to "save face."

So, they're not going to get in there and make themselves look crazy, they are just going to try to save face. They like to be silent when someone else is bringing something up. If they don't agree with it,
they'll still be silent because they like to save face. They don't like public confrontation.

The Arab culture, on the other hand, is sometimes loud and they talk to you very closely. We American's have to have at least six inches of personal space. That's just not going to work well when speaking to Arabs. Remember Arabs do not get loud to make you look bad it's them being who they are.

If we don't understand the different cultural dimensions, misunderstandings can happen quickly. It's important that we understand and learn about the different dimensions. There are a number of websites strictly dedicated to cultures. You can read and learn more.

Q: How does diversity impact an organization?

A: It impacts how people relate to an organization, how they relate to others, to customers and clients, different cultures and the diversity within those cultures, including our own here in the United States. You could either be in for a negative situation or for something spectacular, depending on whether or not you understand the diversity within each culture.

Q: Are diversity and equal opportunity the same thing?

A: No. Again, one is law and one is not law. Equal opportunity is law - Title 7 of the Constitution - U.S. Code Title 10 also deals with equal opportunity. Those are laws.

Diversity, as I have heard it eloquently stated, is not the law, it's the essence of the law. Understand (and I did state before that President Obama signed an Executive Order concerning diversity) that diversity is not enforced by law.

There is one commonality and it is that both are based on merit. Equal opportunity is based on merit. Diversity is based on merit. As long as we treat people based on merit and we treat them fairly, things are good.

We hear people say, "I want equal treatment." You don't want equal treatment. Let me give you an example as to why you don't want equal treatment, but rather fair treatment. Equal treatment would be if the first time I was five minutes late for work because I left a little late and got stuck in traffic, I was treated the same way that my fellow co-worker has been treated after being late four times by 20 minutes or more.

If you want equal treatment for the time he's late and for the five minutes you are late, then knock yourself out. I don't want to be treated the way he should be treated. I want to be treated fairly.

If you understand that example, you will see you don't want to be treated equally either. You want to be treated fairly.

Q: Does an organization need both diversity and equal opportunity?

A: Yes, it does. Again, that's because one is a law and ensures that you are treated in a fair manner. They are both, however, based on merit. You definitely need both.

Q: Why should diversity and human resources be separate?

A: There's a difference. Human resources is law. Diversity is the essence of the law.

Q: What type of diversity training should be done/given in the organization?

A: The type of diversity training organizations need is to first understand the dimensions of diversity; to stress the differences and the fact that everyone is diverse. They also need to understand that it is not just the dimensions, but the different cultures we all come from, how those cultures impact and sometimes rub off on each other, and how you can alleviate or eliminate some of the conflict from those rubs.

3 TEAMS

Q: **Core Concept 3:** Teams - How are team members selected?

A: Team members should be selected based on their talents, their skills, and their ability to work with various individuals. Sometimes

you select them based on how well they bring people together - not necessarily because they know exactly what the team is for, nor because they're really highly skilled in what the team should be, but because they have the ability to create cohesiveness.
That's really what you need in a team. Based on the areas they work in and on their leadership abilities, there are various ways team members can be selected.

Believe it or not, you may want to pick people who can stir up a little conflict. Conflict can be good because it can bring out ideas that will never come out if everybody is there saying, " oh, you're so good," " you're so nice," " that's a wonderful idea." You can get what they call the Abilene Paradox, where pretty much everybody agrees to go down this road because they're so nice, but that's not where you wanted to go. That's a good source too.

If you're not familiar with teams and how they can take the wrong path quickly, I would definitely get the DVD the Abilene Paradox. It's really good for teams. You just need to make sure your team has the people you need and to remember that sometimes you don't pick them for their skills; you actually pick them for how they handle people.

Q: What criteria, if any, are used?

A: Again, the criteria is what they can do for the team. You definitely need people who are skilled and talented in the necessary areas, as well as people that can bring more to the team with their unique skills and talents. If you've never been on a team, it may seem foreign to bring people who don't necessarily have the skills that you're looking for.

If you've ever been on a team that didn't have those skills, you'll appreciate and understand that it would have helped a lot to have somebody there who was good people.

Q: Who should be on a team?

A: You definitely need a strong leader. You need people who are not easily swayed and who are kind of like volunteers. You might need to break your team into two, and you should look for people who are willing to volunteer for different positions. There should be someone who's going to write things down, draft the final report, the results and things of that nature.

It is important to have someone who pays attention to detail, a gatekeeper. The gatekeeper is the person who monitors: "Okay, Jim, that sounds good. You spoke for the last 35 minutes. Let's see if we can't get someone else involved in the discussion." It's very important to have a gatekeeper.

Those are the types of people you need to have on the team.

Q: Are teams formed for a specific reason?

A: Teams should be formed for a particular reason because that keeps them focused. That keeps the time down to a minimum. You don't really need a team for a year, and if you do, you need to check your team's process. You need to ensure that you're picking the right people. A team is generally put together for a specific task that has a clear ending.

Q: What are the five stages of a team?

A: You have the forming, storming, norming, performing and the dissolution - when they're disband. Some people call that the death stage of the team - they have to have some kind of closure. You can't just get to the performing stage and call it a day. They need the mourning stage. They need to mourn the end of the team so they can have some closure.

Q: How is a team leader chosen?

A: Team leaders are chosen in various ways. They should have a strong personality, task easily and be able to keep a team on track.

Sometimes a team leader is chosen because they're highly skilled at the task at hand. They can keep the team focused, keeping everything laser smooth - he/she gets straight to the point, they're not going to vary, they're not going to get off track, "this is what we're here to do."

Sometimes a team leader is chosen because they maintain cohesiveness and can keep the team on track. During the storming stage, people will want to go their separate ways. "I don't want to be on this team any more, I'm tired of you people." Blah blah blah.

Pick someone who may not be as technical but can keep people together; someone with a strong personality who can keep the ball rolling.

Q: Why is it important to understand the 'me' in team?

A: How many times have people heard there's no 'I' in team? True, but there is a 'me' in team, and that is as powerful, or more powerful, than the 'I' that's missing.

It relates to the personality we all have. We wonder, "what's in it for me?" The WIIFM station we all like to tune in to periodically. People will want to know what they will get out of participating. Those are viable questions that need to be answered up-front. That needs to be clear from the beginning, before they start the work.   If not, the team can get stuck in the storming stage and will never go any further. You'll end up getting rid of that team and forming another for the same process.

People need to understand what's in it for them - whether they're looking for some glory, they're looking for job accomplishment, they want to be the team leader or because they are just there to learn something new. You need to determine their needs early to ensure they can get what they need out of being part of the team.

Q: If a team is dysfunctional, is it automatically disbanded?

A: No. A team that's dyfunctional doesn't have to be automatically abandoned. You need to figure out what's going on. Is the leader overbearing? Is it somebody who alwys whines because somebody takes their ideas? You definitely need to figure out what's wrong with the team and if it can be salvaged.

Q: How diverse should a team be?

A: Diversity on a team is good because research has shown that the best ideas come from diverse teams. You don't have to have one person from each group represented in your organization. You want diversity so you'll have different ideas and get the best for everyone in the organization.

Q: What are some benefits of having a diverse team?

A: Again, it's having great ideas. It's having a variety of ideas. It's to gather as many different perspectives as you can about the issue you're trying to fix or the problem you're trying to solve. Diversity stirs different types of conflict and gets you better answers.

Q: What are some drawbacks of having a diverse team?

A: Too many ideas. You can't decide which ideas would be the best. That is the biggest hindrance when you have too much diversity on a team.

Q: How are teams focused or refocused?

A: Refocusing and/or focusing a team is actually pretty easy. If you're called in as the supervisor or are the manager who set up this team, the first thing you need to determine is what happened. How did they get off track? See if you can solve the issue by making sure everybody understands the purpose and goals of the team. Reiterate what you are looking for and hopefully they will refocus and get back on track for the rest of the project.

Q: When teams are formed, who develops their guidelines?

A: The leader of the team and the person who formed it should be responsible for developing guidelines. The leader will know the people assigned to the team and can get ideas from them, while the person who formed the team will know what he or she is looking for and develop the guidelines.

Q: Who receives credit for team success?

A: Everyone on the team deserves some type of credit. The person who formed the team and the leader should consult to make sure proper credit is given to the proper people.

Q: How are teams rewarded?

A: The whole team can get the same type of rewards, or, those who contributed the most can get a more significant reward – everyone else following suit. It just depends on what the reward levels are.

Q: When should a team get new members?

A: That is a drastic measure, particularly when the team is in the norming or performing stage. To remove a long-time member of the team and replace him or her with someone who hasn't gone through all the stages is a hard decision that can derail the group. When that new person joins, people have to get to know them, they'll go through some storming again, and that just sets the team back.

Before that decision is made, the team leader and the person who organized the team need to weight the pros and cons about making a move like that.

Q: Who should decide if team members need additional training to be on a team?

A: Additional training. The person who decided they needed a team and organized it. The leader needs to decide (as they're going through) if the team as a whole needs additional training or if it's

just one person. If it's just one person and he or
she is put off to the side, it breaks the team's cohesiveness.

Q: What type of training should teams receive?

A: Teams should receive basic, generic training on how to be good
team members, how to perform and behave on a team, and, if needed,
specifics on what the team is expected to do. That's basically the
amount of training and/or the type of training a team needs.

Q: How often should teams be used?

A: Teams should only be used to work on an issue or a problem
that will affect the entire outcome of the product or service that the
organization is providing.

Q: When should a team be formed?

A: Only when it is necessary and the person in charge, the
senior manager, sees no other way to resolve an issue than by putting
a team together to focus on why something is happening and how it
can be prevented from happening in the future.

4 INTENT VERSUS IMPACT

Q: **Core Concept 4:** Intent versus Impact - How does intent
versus impact happen?

A: Unfortunately, it happens quite easily and on a daily basis. It
happens when someone says something with good intent but the
person it was directed to misunderstands and takes offense. From
there, it goes downhill.

Q: Is it recognized as a source of discontentment, reduced
productivity or customer dissatisfaction?

A: No. It's not recognized immediately as an intent/impact situation. For example, if someone says to another, "Oh, I didn't know you were capable of doing that job," they didn't necessarily mean it as, "I didn't know you had any skills." Yet the person they said it to may have taken it that way.

Now, the person who took it the wrong way may slowly "lay back" on their productivity because they're taking it in. They are thinking,

"I can't believe she just said that to me. How could she say that to me?" They tend to pull back and slowly but surely, their productivity decreases. They have no enthusiasm about the work anymore. It's not instantaneous, it happens slowly. Nobody's going to link the comment to why their productivity is slowing. That's one way that happens.

Another real life example happened in 2012 when Vogue Italia came up with a new earring design and used slavery in the U.S. as their backdrop to promote it.
It didn't go over well in the U.S. Instead of them trying to fix it by researching or talking about it to African Americans and getting suggestions about how to market their product better, they thought they knew how to handle it and tried to fix it, only making it worse.

They ended up having to scrap the whole campaign because of their ignorance and not wanting to consult with anyone.

Their intent was nothing more than to sell some nice jewelry but their impact was horrible and they lost business as a result.

Q: What are some causes of intent versus impact?

A: It can be actions or it can be behaviors. A phrase that people sometimes use without malicious intent but can still offend is, "I don't see color." To say that to those of us who have color is offensive because it's as though they're ignoring who we are. It's like we don't even exist. I am black and that's a huge part of who I am. I understand why they say it. They think they are making it a good thing and they are trying to say, "I don't see you any differently than I see someone else," but this is a huge thing to me.

People need to realize that what they say can impact others. They don't know how impactful it can be.

My response to people, since this is my area of expertise, is often, "when you say that, I take offense to it because I am black. That's a huge part of who I am and when you say that, it means you don't see me." They don't even consider that until I say it and then they're like, "Oh, I never thought about that."

Saying things can be one thing; behaviors are sometimes even more detrimental. An example for that would be a supervisor who is choosing people to work on a project. They avoid someone who is Asian American and fail to explain why certain people were not chosen.

The Asian American wonders, "why wasn't I chosen? Do you think I can't handle it because I am Asian American?" The real reason they didn't pick them is because they don't have the proper skill set. It's wasn't because they're Asian American. Instead of explaining it to the people that were not chosen, they let it go because they don't think anything about it.

Intent impact situations can be caused by things people don't mean. Their intent was good but their impact was not.

Q: Is intent versus impact only verbal comments?

A: No. They're also behaviors.

Q: What type of behaviors comprise intent versus impact?

A: Someone could leave someone out of a selection process and not explain it because they assume they know they don't have the skill set - that it's not because of them being Asian.

Another example: three or four people are discussing a project and one says out loud, "let's go have lunch." They exclude two or three people who are standing there and happen to look the same yet they look different from the people veing invited to lunch. Insteade of the supervisor saying, "The reason why I'm asking them to lunch and not you is because we happen to be in the same bowling league and you guys don't bowl.

So, we're just going out for a quick social lunch," but he says nothing.

The intent was something totally innocent but the impact was great on those who didn't get invited. All it takes is one simple sentence to explain it. Because the impact was hard and harsh, those people might not perform the same way as they did before that situation.

Q: How are organizations affected by intent versus impact?

A: A lack of productivity and commitment. Some people might consider going to work somewhere else where they feel they belong to the organization. It can be devastating to a company and they don't ever realize why.

Q: How are employees, leaders, clients and customers affected by intent versus impact?

A: Customers and clients don't receive the same quality of product. Customer service is definitely impacted because the staff members who were impacted through the process are not as nice, they're not as friendly, and they don't seem to care about the customers anymore. The leaders take impact because they are left with troublesome employees on their hands. The entire work environment can go downhill, ultimately taking a toll on the whole organization.

Q: Is there training available to prevent intent versus impact?

A: There is training available. Go on the internet and search intent impact. There's a lot of material out there. Many resources are available to organizations, but because they aren't attuned to intent impact, they don't know what's out there.

They should try to bring impact to the forefront, look forward, recognize symbols of impact on their employees, their supervisors, their customers or clients, and start training from there.

Q: Why are there so many egregious intent versus impact incidents?

A: I do believe people don't recognize when it happens. You can see it on their faces because our non-verbs are 93% of how we communicate. You can see it on someone's face almost instantneously when you have said or done something that impacts them. Leaders and supervosors must key in on those situations.

Q: Why are there repeat offenders?

A: Yes, because they don't pay attention to the situation. They don't pay attention to their employees' reactions.

Q: Should organizations change their products or services to stop intent versus impact?

A. No, because the products and services are not the issue. It's the employees that become their issues because leaders or managers have not been attuned to their behaviors. They don't notice how they'r impacting their employees' behaviors.

Q: What are some excuses leaders use when they cause an intent versus impact situation?

A: I have heard leaders and managers use some great lines. "Oh, you're so sensitive. Why are you so sensitive?" Or, "I can't believe you took that comment the way you did. I mean, you just need to change how you see things around here." Or, "You take everything wrong. Everything I say to you, you take it absolutely wrong." They blame the employee in every situation.

Q: Why don't organizations take time to research cultures before engaging them via marketing?

A: They think they're always right. They think they know their market just as well as they know themselves. They may know their local market, but this is a global economy and market.

They don't take the time because they think they know better.

Q: How can leaders prepare to speak to their employees, suppliers, clients and customers from different cultures?

A: It's so easy. You can go on the internet and search Asian culture, for example - so much information comes up. You do, however, need to be selective in what websites you visit. Most cultures have their own website and those are reliable. They will give you a pretty good picture of what's going on.

Q: What can organizations and leaders learn from intent versus impact situations?

A: They can learn that they are not infallible and people can take things out of context, and that it's their responsibility to fix it.

Q: What are some actions organizations and leaders can take to remedy intent versus impact?

A: Become more aware of the situations and look for reactions from their employees when they're communicating with them.

Q: Who can leaders turn to for training assistance?

A: There are a number of possibilities for training situations. I would urge them to be diligent in their pursuit of looking for training.

Q: Should organizations ask experts to review their intended marketing plans prior to going live?

A: Absolutely! There is nothing that could help them more than finding experts in and on cultures to communicate with and help them navigate those situations.

Q: Should organizations seek assistance prior to responding to an intent versus impact situation?

A: They should. They can do that on their own through the training and research they have conducted themselves. But, they're going to need some outside assistance if the situation has been ignored for long enough that it has gotten really bad and is impacting the work environment, the customers and clients.

Q: What steps can leaders take to alleviate or prevent intent versus impact situations?

A: Again, they can be more diligent and perceptive of their employee's reactions, taking immediate action when they notice that something wasn't taken properly. In my experience, I have learned to be able to tell by their reactions and facial expressions that something didn't go well. Leaders need to start immediately.

Seek my assistance. Leaders can easily contact me and find out what they should do now. I'm always available and accessible through my website: simpleinnovationsbusinesscoaching.com.

5 DIAMOND PERSPECTIVE

Q: **Core Concept 5:** Diamond Perspective - How many perspectives do people have?

A: Thousands of perspectives. Unfortunately, they forget about other perspectives and only consider one. They become single-minded and single-focused.

Q: Why try to change perspectives rather than beliefs?

A: You can't change people's beliefs. They believe what they believe and if you try to change their beliefs, they cut you off; they don't pay attention to you any more.

Same thing with their minds. You've heard many times, "My mind is made up." Once their mind is made up, it's done; they're not going to budge.

However, changing perspectives is easy because all you're asking them to do is to look at the same situation differently, from a different view, through a different lens. Then you explain this alternate perspective.

So, I'm not asking them - I just leave it at that. Would you be willing to look at it from this lens, this perspective? I don't say, "and then change your mind," or, "change your beliefs." I simply offer it to them. If they're willing to listen, they can make up their own minds.

Q: What are some items used to change perspectives?

A: I give them examples of situations I've been in and how I handled it. I tell them what happened when I looked at it from a different perspective and what successes I had.

An example is the job I had in the Navy as an Equal Opportunity and Diversity Officer when I was on the USS George Washington aircraft carrier. I had the opportunity, whether I wanted it or not, to sit down with racists (by myself) and interview them. I wasn't a big fan of racists then and I can't say I am a fan of racists today. However, I had to change my perspective knowing that I had to talk to them. I couldn't dislike them. I couldn't get anywhere by hating them, so I changed my perspective to say - this is a person who has different beliefs than I do.

I knew I wasn't going to change their minds or their beliefs, but I still offered them a different perspective through the way I talked and behaved toward them. I would ask the question, "Do you think I'm like the person you had in mind?" Then I'd let them answer.

It not only worked most of the time, but it often worked better than I thought it would. That's how I have used different perspectives, including my own.

Q: What doesn't work when trying to change perspectives?

A: It doesn't work to ask them to change their beliefs after asking them to change their perspectives. Again, I can't change anyone's beliefs. If I ask them to change their beliefs, they shut down and all is lost. In review, I never ask someone to change their beliefs, values or minds. I only offer them a different perspective.

Q: How long does it take to change perspectives?

A: For some, not long; for others, it never changes; for many, it takes a little bit of time. It's just depends on the person.

Q: What happens when perspectives change?

A: New worlds open up for the person and what they changed their perspective on, whether it was a situation, or about a person - they change perspectives on different things. It becomes a flow of new ideas for them which impacts their fellow employees and those who work for them - it's a great thing.

Q: What is the diamond analogy?

A: I took quite a few psychology courses that helped me in my work. My first psychology course was Psychology for the Self. It contained a lot of retrospective work, one of which was the diamond analogy. We were all sitting in a classroom in a pretty big circle, and our professor said, "Now, imagine there's a diamond in the centre of the room and you're all looking at the same diamond at the same time. Think about all the things that you see looking at this diamond."

He then asked us to say what we saw. We all imagined and explained what we saw from our perspective and it was amazing. We looked at the same diamond from various viewpoints and each saw something different. I like to use the diamond analogy on people. It's powerful.

Q: At what level of leadership is this analogy used?

A: It's best used with senior managers, middle managers and first line supervisors because they tend to be capable of opening up more than CEOs or business owners.

Q: How effective is the analogy?

A: It is truly effective. They surprise themselves with how effectively it works when they are free to open up. It's a safety zone. They can discuss an imaginary diamond and offer different perspectives. It opens new options for them. I follow up with, "Imagine your employees. What do you see that you can point out that's different for them?"

Q: When is the diamond analogy appropriate?

A: In any situation, believe it or not. You can introduce the diamond in the middle of the room and observe different perspectives.

Q: How often is follow-up conducted when perspectives change?

A: Follow-up is the key to making this diamond analogy effective. Follow-up determines how powerful the exercise was for you and what changes you think you can make using the diamond analogy. Will you use the diamond analogy with your employees and/or the supervisors who work for you? I usually do three months' worth of follow-up. I may do it every two weeks or so just to make sure it is fresh in their minds and that they are benefiting from it.

Q: Is it easy to see an actual perspective change?

A: Absolutely. You can see it in their behavior-that's what the diamond analogy is for. It's for changing behaviors and how you see things. How we view things is illustrated in our behavior.

Q: If a perspective does not initially change, what happens next?

A: If there's no immediate change, or if the person is having difficulty accepting what happened or what can happen, he or she could be experiencing a fear of change. We all have a fear of change - particularly something changing within us. If they say, "I really haven't changed," I talk to them and ask, "Why do you think that is? Did you see different perspectives of the diamond, different areas, different hues, different lights? Did the prisms change for you?" I talk to them about opening up to a change in perspective. If it doesn't happen, it doesn't happen.

Q: How much resistance is trying to change perspectives?

A: That is dependent on people. Sometimes they don't want to change so they're simply not going to - there's a lot of resistance. Other people are so eager for change that it happens at the snap of a finger.

Q: Is there any particular change in perspective that happens first?

A: The first perspective change is usually in the person themselves. They have allowed themselves to be open to a perspective change. Then it flows outward to other people, helping them. When a person's perspectives changes, it alters how they look at a person and enables more changes; a change for that person.

So, they change themselves first, then they outwardly start projecting this onto others.

Q: After one perspective changes, is it easier to change others?

A: Yes. Particularly if the person was open to that perspective change happening. It becomes easy for other perspectives to change.

Q: What other techniques are used to change perspectives?

A: Other than the diamond analogy, you can offer a different perspective. One of the anologies that I often use is, "What is a block for you?" or, "What do you see?" or, "How do you see things now?"

After they respond, I will say, "Well, let me offer a different perspective." I will introduce it and they will go from there, much like they would from the diamond analogy.

Q: How do you know which techniques to use on a person?

A: I don't know which technique will work on a person right off the bat; it depends on my assessment of where they are or where I think a perspective change would help them.

It's a lot of intuitiveness on my part. An example of this is from one of my favorite movies, *To Kill a Mocking Bird,* with Gregory Peck as Attorney Atticus Finch. Atticus is a country lawyer around 1962. He is asked to represent a black man who allegedly assaulted a white woman. His daughter, Scout, is having issues because people are calling her names and talking badly about her father. She actually gets into a fight at school over this.

Scout asks her father, "Well, why are they calling you bad names? I don't understand." He explains what he's doing and the phrase stays with me. It ties in with what this is all about - how I see or determine what would be best for another as far as changing their perspective goes. Atticus tells his daughter, "Scout, you never know another person until you step inside his skin and walk around in it for a while."

Stepping into someone else's skin means actually being that person, seeing their perspectives and understanding things from their point of view. That's what I try to do.

Q: Are there standard techniques?

A: No. There are no standard techniques. Again, you can research this on the web, discuss perspectives and talk about changing perspectives. There are various ways you can do it. What I have found works best for me is using the Atticus Finch analyogy and saying "yes, I want to walk around in someone else's skin to see their perspective." Then I will try to give them a different perspecive - so maybe they can change.

Q: How much time should be spent on each person trying to change his or her perspective?

A: That varies based on the person, how entrenched they are in their existing perspectives, and how much resistance I experience. If they're really resistant, I'm not going to spend much time with them. I'm just going to offer something and move on. If they seem as though they want to change and their perspective can change quickly, then I'll offer them as many suggestions as I think will help them and their organization. I'll help them be successful as well as their employees.

6 RACE

Q: **Core Concept 6:** Race - What is behind race?

A: Race is not just what you see. Race is also the culture behind it and what makes it what it is. In other words, it's me being black - that is my race, my culture also plays a role, along with my beliefs and a number of other things.

Q: Why is it still uncomfortable to talk about race?

A: That's a good question. In this country today, race remains a contentious issue, particularly between blacks and whites. Although we've come a long way, we still only go so far. You can see that in court proceedings – the Zimmerman versus Trayvon Martin case - which is no more than a race issue to most people. They talk, yet they don't think much about what happened. It was, however, presented as a racial case.

There are other cases around race in the courts today. The divide comes down to did he kill him or not. Did the Hispanic kill a black kid or not? Race is still a tough issue in America today.

Q: What is the human race?

A: Good question because we do have a human race. I'm not sure that anybody really knows what the human race is because we still break things down into black, white, Latino, and Asian. We still racially categorize even though we all belong to the human race - because we are all humans. It would be a whole different way of life if we could just get back to the fact that we are all human beings who experience diversity based on race, ethnicity, religion, age, communication styles, thinking styles, and intellectual thinking. We still primarily and unequivocally all belong to the human race.

Q: How does one's race impact their interpersonal relationships?

A: Unfortunately, it definitely impacts our interpersonal relationships because some races just can't get along with others. They are stuck in the 'I'm in the Caucasian' group mindset. A lot of Caucasians still won't get along with blacks and vice versa because of the way we look. There's too much divide based on what you look like rather than taking who we are as people into consideration.

Q: Why is race sometimes used as a shield?

A: We do sometimes use our race as a shield. For example, though I don't do it anymore, I personally have used my race as a shield to avoid dealing with certain Caucasians, Asians or Hispanics. I'll just not deal with it and tell myself that they don't like me anyway because I'm black.

It's important that we step out of that frame of mind and get to know the person who happens to be Caucasian or who happens to be Asian. There was a time when I was shielding myself from an entire population of people just because of the way they look.

Q: What stops leaders from taking appropriate actions toward someone from another race?

A: Oh, the classic race card. "I don't want to say anything bad to them because they're going to pull the race card." I'm not sure what deck of cards they're dealing from or with, but that is detrimental to an organization that is working as a team and trying to set the proper boundaries of right and wrong. It's no longer about whether you are right or wrong, it's " what race are you?" - right or wrong. That sets a terrible double standard and no organization can be successful using double standards.

Q: When is race a factor in the work environment?

A: Race should never be a factor in the work environment, however, I will give you two examples: one where it might be useful and another when it's not good at all. It might sound counterintuitive to my prior statements, but when you are dealing with a situation in which race is going to help you accomplish or overcome a bad situation, it's a good thing. Some customers or clients feel more comfortable talking to someone of the same race - that's their issue. Sometimes you have to use someone of the same race to achieve a successful outcome.

When race is used in a bad situation, it can follow the same premise. You believe that someone, a fellow employee, a supervisor, whomever it is, will only be comfortable talking to someone of their own race. That's not how to do business in an organization and leaders set a bad precedent by doing so.

Leaders need to handle the situation appropriately. If the supervisor needs to be disciplined, then that person's immediate supervisor should discipline them regardless of what their race or ethnicity is. That's how businesses do business.

Q: What can organizations do to make race an easy conversation?

A: They need to start the conversation. That may not sound right or make any sense, but it's a fact. They need to start the conversation because to ignore it, hinders it. You must start the conversation to make it an easy conversation and to eventually feel comfortable talking to someone of a different race. Ask questions - it's okay to ask questions you are totally ignorant about.

Case in point, I have, in my role as a diversity officer, asked people of a different race or ethnic group questions about things I didn't have a clue about. I would ask them for cooking styles I knew nothing about, or clothing they wear for different ceremonies or in different situations. There is nothing wrong with curiosity. Start the conversation, ask questions. Don't ask in a condensing or mocking voice. Be serious. Asking questions works.

Q: How should leaders handle issues around race?

A: Honestly, open and without putting ones race at fault for a situation.

Q: Who should take the lead in promoting positive relationships involving race?

A: As in most cases, the CEO and/or business owner should take the lead in handling any type of issue within the organization. They must show they are willing, able and confident in communicating with anyone in their organization regardless of their religion, race, ethnicity, or sex. Whatever the issue or situation is, they are confident and comfortable in handling it.

Q: How can racial issues outside an organization impact an organization internally?

A: When race happens on the outside, race happens on the inside. Whenever something is going on outside an organization, it will be brought into the organization. The discussions and frustrations are brought into the work environment. When there is a situation, people talk to people who look like them. It's easy to say, "Don't bring that Zimmerman/Martin case in here. Leave that at the door." Not going to happen. Don't disillusion yourself, your leaders or your managers. That's not going to happen. They're going to talk about it.

So, what should you do? Find a way to talk about it during breaks or lunch hours without bringing strife into the organization. Don't just talk amongst yourselves as blacks, Caucasians, Hispanics or Asians. Create an environment amongst all of you - not a divisive environment along racial or ethnic lines. Talk is going to happen. An atmosphere in which everyone can talk about it will make for a cohesive environment.

Q: When employees identify issues concerning race, what should leadership do?

A: Leadership should get involved in the conversation by offering some kind of a forum for those types of issues. I'm not saying to dedicate 30 minutes of every work day toward sessions in which people can just shut down and talk about it, but what I am suggesting is that during the time that employees do talk about it, they create an environment where everyone can be involved in the conversation. I highly suggest saying, "Okay, I know everyone's probably going to be talking about this, so when you're on your breaks, invite everybody to the conversation. When you're at lunch, invite everybody to the table to talk about it." That will show the employees that you do care about the situation and that you're offering a way to bring the organization together.

Q: What type of training is appropriate for race issues?

A: Every type of training you can possibly get. The training should be consistent and periodic. You can't just train about race once and, "Check mark the done box, we're good for that", because you're not. These things will always come up again. There will always be issues along these lines. I wish I could say that that's not true, but it's a reality. They're going to be there - you always need to have training.

The training should not only be completed by supervisors and/or managers, but also by your diversity officer or VP of diversity. Training should also be done by outsiders who have no dog in the fight so they can give it to you straight and without hesitation, offering an outside voice and ear so people can bring things to them that they feel uncomfortable bringing up to someone within the organization.

Q: How often should training be conducted?

A: Periodically. There is no set timeframe like every three months, every six months, or every other month. The training should be consistent and periodic. It's up to the organization to figure out how frequently they will offer the training.

Q: Who should conduct training on race issues?

A: Again, it should be within the organization - diversity officers, VP of diversity, senior managers, supervisors, first line supervisors and outside vendors.

Q: What are some consequences of leaders ignoring race issues?

A: People not working together and slowed productivity. It can affect employee cohesiveness. It will affect customer service and customer loyalty as well as the flow and quality of your products.

Your organization will be broken down, and even if you are still turning a profit and are productive, will you still want to be good and strive to be the best in this global market and workforce? Leaders need to decide.

Q: What are some skills and techniques leaders can use daily to prevent or preempt race issues?

A: Open communications. Free communications. Allow people to be able to express their concerns and their issues (and those need to be acted upon). Everyone should know what is going on and that issues are being addressed.

Q: Should organizations only be concerned with race internally?

A: No. They need to be aware of what's going on in their community because that is where their staff, clients and customers reside. People don't just live at work. They need to be aware of community issues along racial and ethnic lines and know that they are going to be brought into the organization. Preemptive measures are needed. They can also do some type of preemptive strike, if you will, with training on those particular issues.

They can also develop strategies within their organization that can help the community with issues that are happening outside of it.

Q: Can an organization's reputation be damaged by how they do or do not handle race issues?

A: Absolutely! Once an organization's reputation is damaged, smeared, or tainted, it's hard to bounce back. Even as individuals, we know that if reputations are damaged, you have to work hard to get it untarnished. It's a slow process. Leaders of an organization must be concerned with that and should have preemptive measures in place to ensure they handle those issues, fix their reputation and then move on.

Q: How can an organization repair its reputation after race issues occur?

A: They must be proactive. They must head it off at the pass and publicly, internally and if needed, externally, show that they were wrong and are fixing or have fixed the issue. They should say, "This is what we're going to do in the future to ensure that these types of issues do no happen again." They must ensure that if they do arise again thy will handle them more quickly and decisively.

7 COMMUNICATIONS

Q: **Core Concept 7:** Communications - How many people use the simple communication process?

A: Not many. We learn the communication process in grade and middle school. We definitely used it in high school where we learned more about it, yet we often fail to use it. The basic communication process is in code, the sender or the code sends, while the receiver receives it, decodes it, and then sends feedback. That's the loop, however, we don't go through all of that. The encoding is natural when we send it and the decoding is done naturally by the receiver.

There is no loop to send feedback to the sender so they know that the message was received and understood. "This is what I understood and this is what I'm going to do." We don't bother with all that other stuff. We just send and receive. That is where the majority of our miscommunication comes from. We're not paying any attention to it. We send/receive - that's it.

Q: Why are there so many communication misunderstandings?

A: There are so many misunderstandings because we don't do the feedback portion of the loop. The sender has no idea of how a communication was received - and it's the sender's responsiblity, tbelieve it or not, not the receivers'. If you know anything about the communication model, you know it's the sender's responsibility to ensure that the receiver gets and understands the message.

In short, once the sender sends a message, their job is not over. They must ensure the receiver understood it and is going to respond accordingly. That's required if they don't get feedback automatically. If the sender doesn't hear from the receiver, they need to ask, "Did you understand? Paraphrase it for me so I know you understood." Feedback, or the lack of feedback, is the main issue.

Q: Who is responsible for misunderstanding in communication?

A: Again, the sender. The sender may not think it is, but according to the communications model, they are responsible. 98 out of 100 times, the sender does not give feedback or ensure the receipt of feedback.

Q: What percentage of our communications are non-verbal?

A: Ninety-three percent of our communication is non-verbal. It's how we communicate it and how we receive it.

Q: Why is it important to know about non-verbal communications?

A: It's 93% of how we communicate. You've got to understand it. You've got to understand that different cultures have different non-verbs. This is being American. It is up to us to make sure we understand different cultures and their non-verbs and how they understand them.

Just because we are from the U.S. doesn't mean we can go around using our own non-verbs with everyone around us and expect to be understood. That's how businesses lose billions of dollars every year - expecting everybody to communicate verbally and non-verbally just as we do.

Q: Do cultures communicate differently?

A: One of my favorite examples is the way Italians communicate, and although we don't do much business in Italy, we still do business with them. Italians - loud, in your face, lots of non-verbal gestures. That's how they communicate. Well, we speak loudly as well, so that's a commonality we have. But, again, we like our six inches of personal space. "Don't... uh, uh... you're too close, you're too close!"

Since they like to be right up in your face, that's where they're going to be. They also use their hands, We don't really use our hands that much in non-verbal communication. We do use other non-verbs, but not as much with our hands.

We need to understand we cannot back up from someone who likes to be close to us when they communicate because people take offense to that. They're wondering, "Why are you backing up? What's that about?" A business can lose customers at the snap of a finger if they don't maintain the space that they like to be in. So, we have to adapt our communication tendencies. If we want to do business with Italians, we have to adapt our non-verbs and be on the same spectrum as they are.

Another example is the Japanese. Japanese folks are pretty non-verbal and their voices tend to be soft. When we boisterous Americans go up to them and speak loudly in their faces, they will likely feel offended and want to leave.

We need to understand other cultures and their non-verbs because non-verbs also equal the **vibe** and **tone** of our voice - only 7% of our conversations are comprised of the words we use. This means we really need to understand how to converse non-verbally with other cultures or we lose deals.

Q: Why do leaders need to know cultural communications?

A: To make money.

Q: How can cultural communications gone wrong affect an organization?

A: Communications gone wrong... that's bad. Leaders need to understand that. It's unusual for a CEO to go over to another country and do their direct negotiations. However, the managers or VPs they do send need to understand that we cannot be the typical American, if you will. We have got to conform to their communication style to close deals, develop companies, make money, and avoid losing millions and even billions of dollars because we decided to communicate the way we want.

Q: How can an organization's reputation be damaged because of communication miscues?

A: Reputations - the reputation we have, as typical Americans, is that we're loud, we're boisterous, and we don't care about the deal. These are reputations we've earned and if we're not able to come from a different realm as a company, to visit and conform to their method of business, the organization might as well have stayed here in the U.S. because there will be no business conducted without understanding.

I will go back to the Japanese culture that wants to get to know an organization leader on a personal level before conducting business. Well, the average businessman wants to do business. "I don't want to know you. I don't want you to get to know me. I just want you to sign the contract. Let's get this done so I can go back home."

Those two divergent ideas can't stay divergent, and since they're the people who are signing the contract, it is up to the American businessperson to go over there and conform to what they expect and to how they do business.

Q: When communication miscues occur, how can leaders remedy the situation?

A: Bringing it back to America, it's really critical that communication miscues within an organization are cleared up immediately. It goes back to intent and impact, in a sense. If communication miscues are not handled immediately, it affects employees, how they're engaged, they're commitment, and how they're going to perform on the job – it can be detrimental. Communication miscues must be cleared and everybody must be on the same page to make the organization a success.

Q: What should leaders do prior to dealing with different cultures outside their organization?

A: They must study up on how those different cultures handle communication. Like I have said, there are a number of websites to learn from, but you should use resources from the culture itself. Almost every culture has their own particular website. Asia.com and Arabs.com, for example, will have sections on culture and communications. Those are sample sites you want to look for to get accurate information on what you can expect from a particular culture.

Q: When communicating within the organization, should leaders be concerned about miscues?

A: Yes. Within the organization is just as important as outside the organization. Leaders need to be strong communicators when something goes awry, they need to be on it immediately. They want to clear it up so everybody gets back to the business of doing business and not the business of bad relationships inside the organization. It's personal.

Another great movie that some people might think is odd to quote is "The Godfather" part II - Michael said, "This isn't personal. This is strictly business." When you're in a business organization, it is business. You can be personable, but everything is business. This will cut down on a lot of miscues and situations that can upspring from that.

Q: Does a leader have to learn each employee's cultural communication?

A: It would help to understand their culture and the way they communicate, but not in depth. That's almost impossible to do. They just need to learn something about their culture. Learning something about the employee's culture is going to help when you go outside the organization because an Asian culture is an Asian culture - with one difference. You're looking at Asian American cultures and then you're looking at the Asian culture as a whole. There are going to be differences.

Q: Do employees need to know their fellow employee's cultural communication process?

A: It would be helpful but I don't expect employees to try to learn the cultures of their co-workers. Hopefully they know each other well enough personally to know how best to communicate with each other.

Q: What type of training and education is needed to stave off communication miscues?

A: The organization is responsible for all the training and education their employees receive. That includes cultural training and intercultural training. Again, the periodicity is left up to the organization. It should be conducted by people in the organization and also by outside training individuals/experts.

Q: Why do some leaders expect other cultures will automatically communicate as Americans?

A: That is the American's misfortune of thinking we're the greatest culture ever - if you will, a typical American. You can go to a lot of countries and they'll expect you to be the typical American - loud, boisterous, in need of all of the attention, thinks they know everything about everything and everyone. That's the stereotype we unfortunately live up to. A lot of businesses live up to this stereotype and sometimes it's hard to break - but it can be broken. It's easy to break once you have the proper training.

Q: Is it easy to learn the communication styles of other cultures?

A: Absolutely! Training and education - those are two different things; training is actually doing something and education is nothing more than obtaining the knowledge of how to do something.

Q: Can an organization fix relationship damage by a communication miscue?

A: Yes. Again, it's sometimes a short process, sometimes a long one. It really depends on the people in charge of the organization, how willing they are to admit they have done something wrong and how motivated they are to fix it and move on.

Q: How often should organizations receive cultural communication training?

A: As often as they need it and, again, they must decide the periodicity at which it is needed.

Q: Do organizations need periodic communication training?

A: Yes, they do.

Q: Why did you write this book?

A: Based on my experience in the Navy, I know there is a need out there. The Navy is just a small microcosm of society. I knew that there weren't any books that focused on the issues I am addressing and that it was necessary. To be successful as an individual and as an organization, people need to know that the global view that we have is sometimes skewed and is not as full as it should be. Everyone should understand that diversity is not about what you see, it's about a whole lot more.

Q: What concepts do you want to leave with your target audience?

A: I want them to understand that diversity is definitely more than what they see. Once they understand that, they will be amazed and will hunger for more knowledge about cultures other than their own. I also want to leave them with an understanding of the true global view, and that includes America as part of the global view and market. To be a truly successful organization, they must consider the global view in its entirety, understand what it encompasses and how they can be a player in the global marketplace.

Q: What do others, peers/clients, say about you?

A: Wow... Some of them think I see too big of a picture, that I want too much for organizations and individuals. But I tell them I don't want too much, I just expect them to be able to imagine a bigger picture for themselves.

Others say that I'm very passionate and enthusiastic about diversity. That's true, I am. It is my passion. It has been for 19 years now and I see it growing more. I love what I do.

People also say that I have a deep desire for and hold a space for people who aren't as passionate as I am about diversity. I do. I hold that space for people because I know, I truly know, that once they step into this space and they understand the power of diversity and the global view, they will extend themselves and become so much more than they are. There's nothing wrong with the way they are now, but they'll become so much more - they'll be enthusiastic too.

Q: What do others say about the book?

A: Well, the people I've contacted say that the book is going to be revolutionary and that people will get a lot from it. They say it will change people's lives. It will change the way organizations do business and that will impact customers, clients, and suppliers - anyone who reads the book. People can't wait to read it. They think I have a lot to share and are looking forward to the changes that will come from others reading it. They know I will be a success with this book because I have so much inside me, so much that should be shared with others - that I shouldn't keep to myself.

Q: Who is this book for?

A: This book is definitely for leaders, CEOs, Business Owners, and senior managers in businesses that want to take their company to the next level, that want to be phenomenally successful in the global workforce and in the global marketplace.

Q: Who is this book dedicated to?

A: Wow. This book is dedicated to quite a few people; to my husband who's supported me in all my business endeavors and who supports me every day in what I'm doing. He believes in me and he encourages me.

This book is also for Scott Benning, one of my leaders on the USS George Washington. He played a large part in my improved leadership and my advancement in rank. He made my job easier and allowed me to be myself.

I also dedicate this book to my brother, Marvin. He died not too long ago and was courageous until the end. He showed me how to be strong when my future is uncertain, and to pray to God regardless of how things are going. I will always remember him and what he shared with me.

Q: Who helped you with the creation of this book?

A: Who helped me with the creation of the book? There were at least three or four people who kept telling me I should write one. They just kept saying, "You have so much to offer and so much to share, you should really share it in a book." I am finally writing my book.

A: Who are you and why are you qualified to write this book?

Q: I'm qualified to write this book because of my 19 years of experience in the diversity and equal opportunity field. I have experienced so much through speaking to people who believe that people like myself, black females, have no worth in this world. I know I have worth. I've made some critical changes in the lives of others and they've told me that. They've thanked me for my assistance with that.

I also know what I can give to people and what I have already given. I know how to make their worlds rock even more than they already do. I know that I'm the one to write this book at this time.

PART II
ELLEN TORBERT

Q: Hello, I am Tresté Loving and I am the author of Global Dimensions - Global Dimensions: The Super 7 of Global Success. Today I am going to interview a very dynamic leader in the area of diversity and inclusion. Her name is Ellen Torbert and I will let her introduce herself. Hi Ellen, how are you?

A: Hi, I'm Ellen Torbert, Vice President of Diversity and Inclusion for Southwest Airlines. I'm really excited about the opportunity to talk with you today.

Q: Thank you Ellen. I'm truly looking forward to this as well, because this is going to be great information, not only for myself, but also for the book. It will give me some good background in real time data, if you will, on what's going on out there in the diversity and inclusion world.

The first question is: what skills and expertise do you think I have to write this type of book?

A: First of all, you are truly a visionary. When I first started having conversations with you it was at the very start of my role as a diversity and inclusion officer for Southwest Airlines. You asked me some very strong and thought-provoking questions. You first wanted to know what our ultimate vision was and where we believe we stand on this journey.

You really helped me understand that strategically, we need to have a plan. We also truly need to understand what diversity and inclusion are and how they apply to the business world because it is critical. You are great at driving thought and giving guidance based on where we want to be moving forward.

You are also excellent at really listening and understanding a situation's full picture, where we are mentally and emotionally with what our goals are and how we're going to drive toward them. Additionally, you very diplomatically help us to maintain our focuses by understanding that it is a journey, being patient with us, and then discussing potential challenges and milestone moments. You basically set up a plan that we can appreciate when we have accomplished certain steps.

Q: Awesome, thank you so much Ellen. Do you have any examples of issues that you have actually witnessed or that you have been a part of at Southwest Airlines that you believe I would have been able to help you handle?

A: Oh, definitely. It is the beginning of the journey for us as Southwest Airlines. However, because of our current culture of caring about people and being known to always offer excellent customer service both internally and externally, it can be a challenge to bring in something new when people feel like we're already doing it right.

They might wonder why we even need to take diversity and inclusion into consideration. I believe that you have the insight, experience and background necessary to understand corporate America. You understand the executive leadership rank, the senior leadership rank and the frontline leaders, as well as our frontline employees.

You understand that there are opportunities to bring groups together and have one vision, and you know what it takes in order for us to get there.

So, you should be able to come into an organization at the beginning or in the middle of the journey and find that it is continuous. Depending on where we are with it, you have the experience, the background, the knowledge; you have the perspective to help us to continue driving ahead.

In terms of Southwest Airlines, you helped me understand what the business needs. You helped me with what you called your K.A.T.S.U.P. statement. It's about knowledge, ability, talent, skills, and unique perspective.

That was over a year ago; to this day, our organization understands that, they repeat it, and they know what it means; you were able to help me simplify it yet keep it relevant to what it's all about and how we are going to be able to forge ahead on this journey.

So, I believe you have the talent regardless of where the organization is, to be able to come in and help them to advance; in reality, this way of life is not a project or a mission. I learned that from you early on, in addition to the fact that it will be never-ending if we continue to progress. Based on where our country is, our organizations are our internal employees - there, both internally and externally, they need to focus on creating a truly inclusive environment.

I've learned from you where people are truly valued and appreciated and how you can really celebrate and acknowledge them.

Q: It sounds like Southwest is really moving forward with their efforts and I just want to acknowledge you here in regard to the Rosa Park Award that you received. As I recall, it was an industry award for transportation and you won. Like you said, you were new to the diversity and inclusion arena, but you picked up on it really quickly and have been moving Southwest in the right direction, where others - your peers - see it too.

Congratulations on a remarkable accomplishment!

A: Thank you. Again, I can't say enough about how you have helped me be able to start building a truly solid foundation, and for even being in the position to be recognized for that award. So, thank you for helping me. I still constantly come back to you to pick your brain, just to get additional thoughts as we move forward because it's challenging.

I have found this to be some of the most exciting work that I have ever done in my life, and I have been with Southwest for 26 years on the operations side. This has all happened in the last year and a half, and this is just an amazing world of diversity and inclusion.

Q: Yes it is, and thank you so much for your thanks. Even though you don't work directly with me, what type of leader do you think I am?

A: You are dynamic in the way you communicate and how you envision opportunity and success for the individuals you are communicating with, talking with, and observing. You have a passion for this and I think that is so critical – that you not only have the academic knowledge, but this truly comes from your heart.

That's what I have found when talking to individuals about diversity and inclusion; if you don't have a passion for it, you're not going to be able to sincerely influence others. You are excellent at building relationships and you understand what it takes to build good, strong, meaningful working relationships. You are a very intelligent and sharp individual that is exetremely knowledgeable in this area. I can't say enough about the experience that you have from the military over time. You talk about a world of diversity and opportunity for diversity in the way of generational differences as well as racial and gender diversity opportunities.

You have first-hand experience with that and I have found there to be an acceptance of the information coming from an individual like yourself. You are extremely valuable in bringing credibility to the world of diversity and inclusion.

Q: Great. Thank you very much. You've said so much and I appreciate that. For my final question, would you recommend me to an organization as an equal opportunity/diversity officer?

A: Yes. Without a doubt. You're asking if I would recommend you?

Q: Yes, like as a consultant as far as dealing with equal opportunity and diversity.

A: Without a doubt. I would recommend you in a second and endorse you to the fullest because I know that any organization would greatly benefit from your knowledge, experience and insight. You look at everything as an opportunity, not a problem; an opportunity to get better and to advance.

You really understand the benefits of diverse talent, how to go about seeking that, developing it, and you know that it all results in the bottom line for an organization. You are aware that it is business imperative that we not only understand diversity and inclusion, but that we know how to implement it and how to create this environment where it is truly a way of life. I have found that in order to be competitive organizationally, whether non-profit or for profit, we must understand, accept, appreciate and champion diversity and inclusion. You, without a doubt, understand all aspects of that.

Q: Well, I thank you Ellen, and thank you so much for taking time out of your busy schedule. I know you're very busy at Southwest, and I truly appreciate what you've offered me and what you've offered my readers. I'm sure they will get a lot out of this, so again, I thank you so much.

PART III
SCOTT BENNING

Q: Hi, this is Tresté Loving and I'm the author of the book, *Global dimensions: The Super 7 of Global Success.* Here with me this evening is Scott Benning. Welcome, Scott.

A: Thank you, Tresté. Thanks for having me.

Q: So, how do you know me?

A: Currently, I am a government service employee for the department of the Navy, but have recently retired. So, to walk backwards a little bit, I'm a retired Fleet **Master** Chief in the Navy and happened to work for the Chief Naval Personnel. One of the responsibilities we had was diversity and inclusion. There were many other things on top of that, but we're basically the HR for the Navy.

How do I know you, Tresté? Of course, during our time on board the USS George Washington. I checked on board as the Command Master Chief, and of course, you were the Equal Opportunity Adviser. We put a plan in place and executed a great program under your leadership. It was a great time in the life of that ship, and I think you played a key role in making sure that we enabled great success there.

Q: Thank you, Scott. I truly appreciate it. It sounds like you have moved on to even bigger things outside the Navy. Congratulations on that.

A: Thank you.

Q: What skills and expertise would you say I have to write this type of book?

A: The experience that you brought to the George Washington as an Equal Opportunity Adviser, and your ability to see that position as a tool to train others rather than reacting to ongoing situations. Your experience getting a crew of 3,000–5,000 people, depending on the embarked crew, working at very senior levels in the organization; liaising with department heads and Executive Command leadership; growing awareness of and educating everybody about the importance of diversity in the workforce.

Also, in regard to equal opportunity, you made sure that we stayed in front of those issues rather than having to react to a major situation. You would engage those situations early, get the leadership involved, and work very quickly to resolve any issue before it got completely out of hand.

What I saw there was an entire environment that initially viewed the Equal Opportunity Adviser as somebody who was poking at him or her, and eventually found a leader that was there to help them. That was you, Tresté. You did a great deal to turn that environment around. Ultimately, I think that people realized the value of your leadership.

You're a phenomenal speaker, and so the training evolutions that you put in place were entertaining for people to actually understand the message. You're a very good connector in your public speaking, and you do it very well, making it fun for everybody.

Those are great qualities. Your experience along with your ability to have a vision, to make a plan that influences leadership to go a certain direction, to put a plan in place and execute it, and to be the right kind of leader and speaker - I think those are all great qualities that you have.

Q: Thanks, Scott. I appreciate that. Do you have an example of a situation that seemed kind of difficult, but with my help and guidance, was resolved?

A: Well, I don't recall one specifically and I don't know want to use specifics to a certain point because of individuals involved.

I do remember cases in which people would think that they were being discriminated against - whether it would be gender or ethnic discrimination - when really what you had was a failure to communicate.

You were able to sit with the person that felt discriminated against, educate them, then approach leadership to help them understand how that person felt and how they could close the gap through stronger and more effective communication. It would ultimately remove a lot of that tension.

I think through the entire process, that was one of the tremendous values – your strength in the communication effort.

I think that ultimately helped us to get leadership to understand people, and for the people that worked for the leadership to value and respect them. Respect became a two-way street. A strengthening of the organization through the relationship and the communications.

Q: That's a great example that will actually go well with one of the chapters in the book. So awesome. You mentioned a little bit about my leadership. Is there be anything that you'd like to add about the type of leader I was?

A: Well, you are very positive. I think that in that type of position, you can get yourself to a place where you are perceived as negative because all that people hear are complaints, as opposed to understanding that you have to work at different levels of the organization, you have to be able to connect with people at different levels to get them to understand what's actually going on, and then be able to close that gap.

To be able to do that at multiple levels, to be able to understand the most junior person in the organization and get them to grasp something... it's influence, it's leadership and the way that you understand the way others are understanding the message is a unique quality.

There are great examples in history in which people can tell stories to get people to understand things, and that's one of your qualities that is of great value. You are able to connect and communicate with people and get them to understand things through stories, that they understand through their level and through their background, that they can best connect with and move forward and grow from.

Q: What value would I have to an organization?

A: The value is in your experience, your energy, and your ability to communicate well. There are very few places in which somebody can say that they worked in an environment in which people lived 24/7. The level of situations that that could create is probably much more dynamic than in a corporate workplace.

You were able to understand the relationships at that level and how they can affect the workplace, and then took it to a place where someone works eight hours a day during the week and understood the sensitivities, the many relationships and how they were impacted by a lack of effective communication (when oftentimes it is just a misunderstanding).

You were able to close that gap for people and educate them about understanding somebody else's background and how they might receive something differently than another. You have obviously done a lot of research and exercising of that leadership skill in the actual environment.

It is valuable to have someone that has that experience to come into a company and be able to make leaders more effective. It's also valuable to be able to understand that leadership is at all levels, to the point that you can take somebody in the middle or somebody at the bottom of the organization and make them understand that they have a leadership responsibility too.

It's called effective communication – up the chain as well as down the chain. Your ability to educate other people and communicate effectively with them will strengthen an organization, and you've dealt with many of those things in the past already. I think that you'd be a great asset to anybody that you were out there helping.

Q: The last question I have is: Would you recommend me to an organization as an equal opportunity and/or diversity officer consultant?

A: Absolutely. I've seen others in the Navy-wide organization that were doing that job, and we've talked before. You'd be perfect for one of those jobs. I think you would do very well working for a Navy-wide organization with access to 300,000 people. You'd be a phenomenal adviser for senior leadership and would be able to oversee an entire program and get it effectively executed throughout a large organization. So, I would absolutely recommend you.

Q: Scott, that's all I have for you, and let me give you my biggest thanks for offering your valuable time to sit down and talk with me. I really appreciate your support and you will definitely be one of the people mentioned in the book. You can buy it for all your friends or something!

A: There you go!

Q: Thank you so much, Scott, I truly appreciate it.

A: Thank you for everything and best wishes with the book. I look forward to buying plenty of copies. Not because my name's in it, but because you're writing it.

Q: Okay, thank you.

PART IV
RENÉE FULLER

Q: Good afternoon. I'm Tresté Loving and I am writing the book, *Global Dimensions: The Super 7 to Global Success.* This evening I am speaking to a very good friend of mine, Renée Fuller. Welcome Renée and thanks so much for joining me.

A: Thank you.

Q: Would you please tell everyone who you are, what you do and how you know me?

A: Okay, my name is Renée Fuller. I'm currently an investigator with the Navy Reserve Inspector General Office. I met Tresté 11 years ago, May 2002 roughly, when I checked on board the USS

George Washington, CVN 73. I was the legal chief at that time and we worked closely together with conducting investigations and sometimes interviews.

Q: Could you tell me a little bit more about what our specific positions were and how they were correlated with our roles on the George Washington?

A: On the George Washington, I was the legal chief for the legal office in the brig on board the ship, and Tresté worked as the Equal Opportunities Advisor. She was a chief when I first met her and eventually became a senior chief. We dealt with a lot of diversity on board the ship: race, religion, gender... we even had skinheads. There was a lot of sexual harassment. We had cases that dealt with just about everything - **fraternization;** and during that time we had to take the individual to Executive Officer Enquiry where the XO ask the questions and Tresté was always there for all the XOI' is Executive Officer Enquiry and always there for the Captain during Captain's Mast.

So, if the Captain or the Executive Officer had questions pertaining to that or if she investigated or interviewed the individual,

Tresté was right there to answer any questions.

Q: What skills and expertise do I have that make me qualified to write this book? We're talking about culture and strategies as far as diversity and inclusion.

A: Tresté enjoys reading, she is a great writer, wonderful listenter, and communicator, and is excellent with grammar. She's writing about what she knows. I think she's confident in her writing ability and she has tough skin for any criticism that comes her way. She works hard and she has a great imagination.

Q: What specific example(s) can you give about a difficult situation that she actually handled that you were either a part of or that you knew of on the ship?

A: I'm not sure of the case, but I do remember a situation involving a Caucasian male that was a skinhead. His job was as a damage control man on board the ship. He was responsible if some type of fire or any type casualty broke out on board the ship. I mean, he was responsible for saving us. As I mentioned, he was Caucasian and Tresté is an African American woman. He didn't like blacks, but she sat down in front of that individual and spoke to him like there were no boundaries, no issue of race. He was just a human being and he responded to her which was really shocking because he told our Executive Officer that if there was a fire, he would not save her, he would let her die.

Nonetheless, she was able to be professional and sat down with him and asked him questions about why he felt that way and why he did certain things. I felt that was very professional of her. I don't know if I could have been able to do that. But, she's always like that; calm, nothing bothers her. She's open.

Q: Yeah, I remember that story myself. What type of leader would you say that Tresté is?

A: She is participative and she believes in working together to solve the problem. She likes to include her people or whoever she's working with in the decision- making process. I'm sure there are times when she has to be the leader. I think it depends on the situation. If she had to be put in that situation, I'm sure she could be a different leader, but she does have a combination of both.

Q: Okay. Would you say that she is reactive or proactive?

A: I think she's more proactive. Tresté thinks about what to do if an event happens. She doesn't wait for the event and she doesn't let the event catch her by surprise.

Q: How valuable would you say she is to an organization?

A: She's very valuable. She an exceptional leader. She believes in confronting the issues head-on and providing you with feedback to correct the issues if necessary. I think she's an outstanding communicator, counselor and role model. She's an innovative problem solver and a mediator; she has been used as a mediator several times. I think she's great for any organization, they would be very lucky to have her.

Q: That was actually the last question, would you recommend her to an organization as an Equal Opportunity person and/or diversity consultant? Would you recommend her for one or both?

A: Both of those. She's provided plenty of Equal Opportunity advisors in training on the George Washington which had over 7,500 sailors. She played a key role in the command [20.38] and addressed potential Equal Opportunities problems. So, yes, I would recommend her.

Q: Does she work well with senior leaders as well as junior employees?

A: Yes. Tresté isn't going to treat you differently if you are a captain. Yes, she does respect the collar devices and rank, but if you did something wrong, she will hold you accountable regardless of your position.

Q: Renée, I truly thank you for being honest with your responses today and for providing such great insight. I appreciate your time and I look forward to speaking to you again, maybe on a follow-up book. Thank you very much.

A: You're welcome.

Q: **Thanks** Renée **again like I truly, truly appreciate it because the instances, actually one of them I didn't use with my little fireman. I did use some others though and I forgot about my little favorite little boy there, I can't believe I forgot that when he was going to leave me burning. I can't believe I forgot, he was going to leave me burning.**

PART V
GARY HILL

Q: My name is Tresté Loving and I am the author of *Global Dimensions: The Super 7 of Global Success*. I'm here today with Gary Hill.

Hi Gary, thanks for agreeing to be interviewed.

A: Hi, Tresté. I'm glad to be here.

Q: Thanks. Tell me a little bit about yourself and what you do.

A: As Tresté mentioned, my name is Gary Hill. I retired from the Navy back in 2002 after serving for 24 years. I retired as a Navy Chief. I now work for the Department of Defense, working within the intelligence community. I work for the Office of the Inspector General as the Staff Director within the Department.

I've been with the Office of the Inspector General for three years. I've been with the Department of Defense going on a total of 34 years. So, service is kind of my background.

Q: Great. Can you tell us how you know me and for how long?

A: I've known Tresté close to 18 years now. I met her when she became part of the organization that I was working for, the Navy Leadership Training Unit (NLTU) Detachment in Washington DC. Tresté was one of the facilitators there and I met her and have known her since then.

Q: Can you tell us what I was doing and how we worked together?

A: Tresté was one of the facilitators teaching Navy Leadership to sailors; helping sailors become more efficient in their leadership skills as well as becoming more efficient Managers.

We provided a series of lectures and courses designed, again, to enhance their proficiency skills. Tresté came onboard first as a Junior Facilitator before she quickly by-passed not only myself but also the Chief at the time.

Tresté was one of the key leaders within the Navy when they wanted to facilitate and educate people and hone their efficiency skills, leadership and management.

Q: What other skills and expertise do you know me to have?

A: The other skills and expertise that I know you to have are relevant to the skills that I had prior to becoming a Navy Leadership Facilitator, as I came to the Navy Leadership Facility after being an Equal Opportunity Advisor.

When I was transferring from being a Navy Leader, I spoke to Tresté about becoming an Equal Opportunity Advisor. She took that on and has done an admirable job as a Navy Equal Opportunity Advisor.

She was an Equal Opportunity Advisor at a number of organizations and at each one she was chiefly responsible for letting management know how equal opportunity equates to mission effectiveness.

Q: Great. Do you think those skills and expertise that I had there qualify me to write this book?

A: Absolutely. Not only qualified to write a book, but more qualified as a proficient individual, training organizations and providing lectures to senior leaders on how important it is to be more cognizant of performance management as it equates to operational efficiencies.

One of the important aspects of that is understanding the culture of an organization. Without understanding an organization's culture, it'll be harder for it to recognize how the could improve their efficiencies if they do not leverage or understand the organizational culture.

Q: Do you have an example of an issue that I have either handled or that I could handle along the lines of equal opportunity or diversity?

A: Certainly. One of the things that really separates Tresté from other colleagues and peers of the Navy Facilitators and Chiefs within the Chiefs Community, was her ability to identify an individual's weaknesses and work with them to correct that deficiency.

But also, Tresté was never one to let one go, simply by the fact that they were just a peer.

One example is knowing a fellow facilitator was lacking certain skill traits which were very important for facilitating a number of sailors about ways that they needed to be effective as leaders.

But, this particular facilitator lacked certain knowledge in that area or failed to thoroughly research what was necessary to be able to comfortably and confidently facilitate an audience.

Others would have simply let that individual go by and work with that person and then over time, that individual probably would have assessed or amassed the abilities to do that. But, the costs would have been those that he or she incorrectly facilitated to, possibly resulting in more of a detriment.

Tresté was quite poignant about bringing it to that person's attention and stood her ground in identifying that weakness. She was quite direct in what that individual needed to do to bring up that skill set.

The end result was that the person did it; they put in a lot of hard work to do it; there was a degree of consternation over the fact that the person felt that they should have still been able to teach though they were not fully proficient in doing it.

That's not Tresté's forte. Tresté wants to ensure that anyone that she comes in contact with and that she has a responsibility for is doing well and has all their weaknesses pointed out so that their skill set is improved enough to get a passing grade.

Q: Do you think I am reactive or proactive?

A: It's situational; when it comes to leadership, she is primarily proactive. When there is a problem, she is reactive. She has great analytical skills and she can look at what the issue is, focus on the causes and then come up with recommendations for preventative steps for the organization to implement to avoid future occurrences.

Then, from a proactive stand-point, she is great at going into organizations and talking proactively about programs and projects and how one can improve those efficiencies.

Q: My final question is: Would you recommend me to an organization as an Equal Opportunity Office or a Diversity Officer/Consultant?

A: Absolutely. One of the things that separates Tresté from a lot of people is her experience. She has vast Navy experience as a Leader, as a Manager, as a Facilitator and as a Coach in a number of disciplines.

To be a Navy Leader onboard an Aircraft Carrier that consisted of over 5,000 people and be the Principal Manager of that organization's Equal Opportunity Program gives her the confidence and the competence of doing a thorough job.

Additionally, she is able to focus on small organizations; gathering senior leaders within those organizations and talking to them about the importance of program management with performance management for the efficiencies of an organization.

She certainly has the skill sets to be able to write a book; to be able to have that book published and be used by organizations to help their efforts of enhancing their diversity skills.

One of the things that I think is important to state is that when she was playing the role of an EO Advisor, she did a number of things that I'm presently doing now from an Inspector General's standpoint. She was identified by the Inspector General of the Navy to assist the improvement of their abilities and go into organizations.

The role of an Inspector General is to look into an organization to help it improve its efficiencies through independent and objective oversight, foresight and insight of their programs and operations.

Tresté was able to do that and the benefit was to improve organizational efficiencies. So, she is certainly one that could enable an organization to improve its efficiencies through a book or visiting businesses to give a series of lectures, or coaching one-on-one workshops. She has the ability easily to help an organization grow.

Q: Okay, great. Thank you Gary Hill, I appreciate your time today.

A: Thank you.

PART VI
DEE BUIE

Q: Hi, I'm Tresté Loving and I am the author of the book *Global Dimensions: The Super 7 of Global Success.* Today I'm interviewing Delores, better known as Dee Buie, and she will be helping me with a section of my book. So, hello Dee.

A: Hi, how are you?

Q: Good. We're going to get started with the first question: How do you know me?

A: Well, many years ago, in 2002 or 2001, I met Tresté on board the USS George Washington. I guess we started our relationship via telephone prior to actually meeting each other. I was going to be stationed at sea duty for approximately three years and she was my sponsor, indirectly. She was the one to get me involved with what was going on, to explain the culture of the ship, expectations, and greet me - gave me a tour of what was going on and what to expect once I got there. That relationship evolved over the years into a deep friendship.

We still communicate professionally and personally. She's more family than friend, in a sense; that's what she has become. That's where she fits into my life.

Q: Can you elaborate a little bit about what your position on the ship was?

A: When I initially boarded the George Washington, at the time I was the Senior Chief Petty Officer coming on board as the lead Navy Career Counselor. Eventually, within a year and a half/two years, I became the Master Chief on board and with that position, Master Chief Navy Career Counselor, again, in charge of five other shipmates.

I worked hand-in-hand with Tresté and several other key individuals including CO, Commanding Officer, Executive Officer as well as the Command Master Chief, aligning and ensuring the culture of the ship's diversity, making sure things ran smoothly and people knew where to go and to get information.

Overall, my job was to get a feel the pulse of the ship, any information coming in, any new programs the Navy was bringing on board or removing or taking away from; I had to have the knowledge of all of it and pass that information to the personnel on board.

Q: Could you describe your current position?

A: Currently, retired military. I did 29 years active duty, and as a matter of fact, was able to get this position through a recommendation from Tresté. So, with that recommendation, I was initially hired to get into curriculum development, but took on a different role, manpower training, one of the senior research analysts here, and still worked with the military indirectly.

Our job here is to ensure that all personnel are trained on all equipment and/or systems going on board naval vessels in advance. They need to have that knowledge prior to reporting so that they will know what to do once they arrive.

Q: For the next question: What skills and expertise do I have?

A: Oh geez.

Q: Let me rephrase that question, I'm sorry. What skills and expertise do I have to write this book?

A: Wow. Three/three and a half years on board George Washington as Equal Opportunity Officer. She was the go-to person for most of the information coming in - anything that had to do with equality; right, wrong, indifference, sexual harassment, etc. She worked hand-in-hand with the legal department.

She was the pulse, in a sense. The person I went to to ensure that fairness was maintained on board. She had the ability to know the dos and don'ts as far as management was concerned, which should not be done with personnel before and making sure that they're actually getting that information to them.

Q: Do you have an example of a difficult situation that I actually handled?

A: Yes, there are so many. We had several racial incidents on board the George Washington that she had to deal with. We had some difficult service members on board, personnel that could be labeled in this day and age as a racist and in one case, I think one came straight on and told her that they didn't care for people of color.

So, she had to sit him down and actually talk to him one-on-one. In the end, it was rather odd. That person will not end up becoming a friend. He was very negative, abusive, against the system, and didn't care for people's color. But, in the end, with Tresté's counseling - despite the racial slurs that she had to endure - he actually conversed with her and liked her.

That was difficult for her. A lot of leadership on board did not want to deal with him, but she actually took that time and sat him down and got through that difficult situation. It was good for the service member as well as some of the senior leadership on the ship because they didn't know how to handle it, since they didn't have the background, the patience and/or the training to deal with it.

Q: What type of leader would you say I am?

A: I would definitely say Tresté has a proactive personality. She looks for solutions for everything that's presented to her - good, bad or indifferent. Even if people say it can't be done, she'll find her way around it. With the cases in which people were labeled as throwaways, so to speak, or people who were difficult or didn't want to take the time because they didn't think they could be saved and/or trained, she maintained a soft spot and the ability and tenacity to stick with them. She wanted to help them change.

That's Tresté in a nutshell. Happy-go-lucky at times, but she has an opinion and will provide you with it whether you want it or not. She also is not easily swayed at all. Small but large in stature, so to speak. She held her own very well considering her position on board the ship. She made a name for herself. People respected her. Folks always seek her out to handle critical situations and diffuse it when it was getting difficult for other folks.

She also doesn't back down very easily and can't be overpowered. She isn't necessarily a person that loves the sound of her voice, but when she does speak, people listen because she has a lot to say and it makes sense. I would say she is definitely proactive, kind but firm, very firm, and aggressive when things need to get done. Task her with something and it's going to get done in a timely manner and she'll do whatever it takes to get the information to you.

Q: Why am I valuable to an organization?

A: Well, the value comes in her title by itself. When it comes to diversity, knowing what the rules and regulations are and what people can and cannot do within limits, she will take the time to make sure that information is put out there.

Tresté has a strong background and very passionate about her job and what she does. She cares about people, so definitely a people person. She even has the ability to bring calmness to the ones that are difficult, and I think her spirituality and the religious aspect of that helps with that. Her belief in her background. Any organization accepting or receiving her would I guess, in a sense, gain from her knowledge and her people will be well taken care of for sure.

Q: So, it sounds like you would recommend me to an organization as a consultant?

A: Most definitely, with the only caveat being that if they want a person that's going to go along with the organization's current status quo, that's not going to happen unless it's within the rules and regulations.

She realizes that there's a grey area, but doesn't necessarily work in that grey area because even though the rules and regulations may say one thing, she realizes that as humans, sometimes you have to look for work that is going to benefit the organization as well as the person involved.

Q: Well, thank you so much Dee. I appreciate your time. Thank you. You said some great things. I truly appreciate it.

A: They're all true. You're good people.

CONCLUSION

Any questions? A Business Owner or CEO wanting to take their organization to a phenomenal level in the global market definitely has the information they need in this book. From Chapter 1 Socialization describing how we got to be who we are today to Chapter 7 Communications.

ABOUT THE AUTHOR

Tresté Loving is a 26 year retiree from the U.S, Navy who has a tremendous passion for people of the globe. This passion created an overwhelming desire for her to serve others in the Equal Opportunity and Diversity/Inclusion profession. Tresté graduated from Strayer University with honors, receiving a Bachelors of Science Degree in International Business. Graduating with distinguished honors from an 18 week Diversity and Equal Opportunity course, Tresté placed second in a class of 100 and received the Distinguished Speaker Award. As an U.S. Navy Equal Opportunity Diversity officer, she received various personal awards throughout her career, creating work environments that increased productivity, reduced discipline, increased talent retention and more.

In today's work environment most of the issues that occur have to do with unfair or disparate treatment and cultural issues ranging from how employees are disciplined to not understanding an employees' culture, or race. Tresté experienced these very issues growing up in a small town of about 500 in Kentucky where the population was about 78% Caucasian, and while living in Western KY. Living in a small town helped Tresté relate to others from different backgrounds, ethnic groups and races. Living in Western KY experiencing racism and racists behaviors Tresté learned how to respond positively in those situations. This equipped her for the Navy and her training; Tresté was unstoppable as a Diversity Officer.

Tresté's experience and training in race issues and other poor work environmental situations was crucial to an organizations' phenomenal results. Her work has been covered in the Washington Post and she has answered many Congressional Inquiries which she handled expertly rendering truthful decisions to both the organization and the individual. She ensured organizations kept focused on their daily operations during these situations.

Tresté's passion is to help every organization be phenomenal in all aspects of their business. She desires to make this a reality in your organization.

Check out her website for the services she offers: www.simpleinnovationsbusinesscoaching.com. You may also reach her at tlovingsimplified@gmail.com.